STRESS TO SUCCESS STORIES

To Inspire Individuals and Businesses to Excel

Hansa Pankhania

Sohum
Publications

Stress to Success Stories

To Inspire Individuals and Businesses to Excel

© Hansa Pankhania 2022

Published 2022

SOHUM PUBLICATIONS

Byfleet, Surrey, England

ISBN: 978-1-914201-14-1

A CIP catalogue record for this title is available
from the British Library.

Cover design: webdirections
www.webdirections.co.uk

STRESS TO SUCCESS STORIES
To Inspire Individuals and Businesses to Excel

11 powerful stories inspired by real life, covering professional and personal challenges, with solutions that will ignite positive changes in your life.

Within these stories, you will find simple yet powerful techniques that will help you to live a stress-free, healthy and energetic life. Each story is accompanied by a handy commentary packed full of expert guidance and tips.

The stories also encourage interventions that will optimise effectiveness and productivity within any business or institution.

Whatever your situation, I feel confident that you will find something in here that will have the power of unleashing positive changes in your work and home life.

Contents

career. That's what happened to Joe Barnes but he got back on track. Find out how he did it in this story.

Malcolm has never heard of mindfulness. He discovers how living mindfully can trigger subtle positive responses that change his life.

The inspiring tale of the transformation of Neil, a senior executive on the verge of a nervous breakdown.

All the tips and techniques are passed on in good faith and the author and publisher are not responsible for any contraindications. Please consult your doctor if in any doubt, before using the techniques.

Foreword

by Professor Derek Mowbray, PhD., FBPsS, FIHSCM
Chairman, The Wellbeing and Performance Group

This is another amazing book by Hansa Pankhania, using the style of storytelling to convey some very serious, yet extremely helpful, advice and support on issues that have the potential for causing distress in us all.

The causes of stress are many and varied. They are often normally accepted behaviours and actions, which have been 'permitted' to happen over time and which are not prevented by the actions of leaders and managers. It is important therefore to equip individuals with the skills and knowledge to respond to such events in ways that reduces their impact.

Storytelling is a brilliant way of conveying serious messages in an easily understandable manner. Stories resonate with us, more so if the story is a close representation of something we have experienced. These stories are each taken from actual events. Learning points are drawn from the story and questions posed to the reader that help cement an understanding of the key messages.

This is another comprehensive and easily accessible book by Hansa that covers a broad range of topics. She brings them to life and uses them to help us cope better with adversity.

Welcome

Every so often there is a story highlighted by the media about stress issues affecting a famous person; 'actress has breakdown', 'international sportsman diagnosed with depression' and so on. The silver lining to these worrying stories is that they raise awareness of the severity of these problems and as a result, perceptions are changing for the better.

Of course, it's not just the rich and famous who experience stress-related issues. Stress is the **number one** cause of workplace absence in the UK. In 2019/20 there were **an estimated 828,000 workers** affected by work-related stress, depression or anxiety. This represents **2,440 per 100,000 workers** and results in an estimated **17.9 million working days lost** (Health and Safety Executive UK).

These figures are shocking; however, I am encouraged to see that, at last, the importance of recognising stress and the need to address the effects stress has on individuals in all areas of their lives is beginning to be taken seriously. For too long we have been reluctant to admit to feeling stressed, for fear of being labelled 'weak'. This stigma is gradually breaking down and more people are seeking help sooner.

There is a raft of self-help books out there that can give you guidance on how to overcome stress and perform at your peak. So why should you read this one as opposed to all the others? It is because this book is not one with dry facts on stress prevention and wellbeing. This collection of workplace short stories is written from experience and inspired by our clients. These stories are based on real-life scenarios and interventions, but I have presented them in a way that protects and respects our client confidentiality.

In this book, I share individual and corporate scenarios inspired by real-life situations to promote more understanding of the triggers of stress and the need to seek help at an early stage. Within the stories, I share simple powerful techniques that will help you to live a stress-free, healthy and energetic life, as well as encouraging corporate interventions that will optimise effectiveness and productivity within any business or institution. Hopefully you will see that the small investment in these interventions saves long-term costs, helping to enhance the bottom line considerably.

As such, it doesn't always mean that at the conclusion of the tale everything is rosy in the garden and everyone lives happily ever after. Real-life isn't like that. However, these stories will resonate with many of you and give you tips and techniques to help overcome common as well as complex problems.

It will also make for an interesting and exciting read.

Welcome

This book is equally relevant for individuals, employees and managers.

I am confident that you will find something in these pages that will give you the power to unleash positive changes in your work and home life.

Please feel free to contact us via www.aumconsultancy.co.uk if we can help in any other way.

The website has FREE resources such as audio and video recordings that will help to galvanise your wellbeing.

Story 1: The Mediator

Paula Hart had always remembered her first lesson at secondary school. It had been a Religious Education class and she could remember her eleven-year-old self, sitting in the stuffy classroom nervously awaiting the arrival of the teacher, Mr Denton. The quiet rumbling of chatter suddenly halted as the door of the room opened and a bearded, middle-aged man strode in. He was wearing a terrible brown suit. He had unbrushed, greasy black hair and his beard revealed that he had cornflakes for breakfast. He walked to the front of the room, picked up a piece of chalk and wrote a sentence on the blackboard:

"God loves you and has a great plan for your life."

Paula was not impressed; the recent death of her rabbit Floss had left her doubting the existence of a higher being. She had no idea how the death of Floss was part of God's 'great plan'.

Mr Denton turned round to the class and stared into the middle distance, raised a finger and uttered one word: "But...". As opening words go from teachers, it was not inspirational by any measures, but the class were young and full of nerves, so they remained silent, attentive and slightly confused. He turned back to the board and wrote a second sentence underneath:

"Everyone has an enemy."

Paula was perplexed; Mr Denton was a very strange man indeed!

Thirty years on and Paula Hart was beginning to change her views on the R.E. teacher's opening gambit. Over the previous few weeks, she had started to be aware that she did indeed have an enemy. That enemy's name was Mo Akhtar and he seemed hell-bent on making Paula miserable, angry and unemployed.

Paula had been the receptionist at Fairville Doctors' Surgery for fifteen years and until recently she had thoroughly enjoyed her job. Her husband was a successful businessman, so she had few financial worries even though her job did not pay that well. Nonetheless, she was helping sick people, making a difference and she genuinely loved talking to the public and making them feel at ease. She was a content, happy and cheerful lady; that was until Mo Akhtar appeared on the scene!

Mo had been appointed as the Office Manager for the surgery. The surgery had never previously had an office manager but in recent times they had become increasingly busy, had taken on extra staff and reached a stage where the partners felt that the staff needed a full-time manager to look after the administration of the surgery. Paula felt the move was pointless. Yes, they were busier, but that just meant everyone had to work slightly harder and chip in to help each other out.

When Mo came along, everything started going downhill for Paula. He was a well-meaning young man, who had previously been an office manager for a private sector firm. The partners felt that his skills were transferable and would help make the surgery a 'well-oiled machine'. Keen, confident and hard-working, Mo proved to be popular with the partners straightaway. However, his methods were not to everyone's liking, especially Paula.

For a start, there were the daily meetings or 'huddles' as Mo called them. The eight members of the admin team got together for fifteen minutes whilst Mo talked them through what was going on in the surgery and asked them questions about how things were going. It was all based around a big whiteboard that charted the performances of everyone in the meeting. "Performance?" Paula said when she first heard about the meetings. "The only performance information you need to know from me is that I'm performing at my best every day!"

Despite the murmurings from Paula and other staff members, the meetings had become a staple of the daily routine. More annoying were the seemingly endless streams of new forms that she had to fill out every day. Elaborate tick lists to demonstrate that she had performed vital tasks such as locking her desk before going home and not leaving any personal items on her desk. It was all work she had always done but now it required filling in a form! Woe betide if she forgot to complete any of her daily tasks, she would be singled out during the following day's 'huddle' and asked to explain herself, an experience Paula found to be extremely humiliating.

Even more humiliating were Mo's regular visits to the front desk. He would sit and observe Paula dealing with patients for fifteen minutes then spend a similar amount of time offering suggestions as to how she should improve her patient service technique.

"I've been doing this for fifteen years and never had a single complaint," Paula would say.

To which Mo would respond with a curt, "There's always room for improvement."

This would often lead to Paula storming into Mo's office later in the day and the two of them engaging in a shouting match that had no real prospect of a result. Paula had taken the matter to the partners, but as Mo was producing good results, they did not take her concerns seriously.

For Paula, these incidents were greatly upsetting. She was venting her frustrations outside of work, usually at her husband Matt. They had had numerous arguments over the last few months and Paula was worried that she was driving him away. She was also struggling to sleep, as the prospect of coming to work was filling her with dread.

"Penny for them." Paula had been in the tea room at work, daydreaming for about ten minutes, lost in her own world of turmoil and stress. Her train of thought had been broken by her colleague Jilly. Jilly was also unhappy about the changes Mo had introduced but she was a far more reserved person than Paula and just got on with her work without actively complaining.

"They're not worth a penny," replied Paula. "I was just thinking about how horrible it is working here now!"

Jilly sighed. "I know what you mean, but I guess that's just how it is here now. We had it good before. Now we've got to be all modern and do all the weird corporate things."

"I wish I could accept that, but I can't. He talks to me like I'm a child; he's tearing this place apart. It used to be full of happy workers, now everyone wanders around looking miserable and grumbling to themselves. It must be terrible for patients. If it goes on much longer, I'm just going to walk out!"

"You don't really mean that."

"Watch me! I don't need this. We can get by on Matt's income until I find a new job."

At that moment, Mo Akhtar walked into the tea room. "Afternoon, ladies," he said cheerily. "Hope you all had a great weekend."

"Yes, thank you," said Paula in a flat tone, before making her excuses and leaving the room. She worried, "What's happening to me? I can't stand being in the same room as the man, and that's not like me at all."

That evening, Paula went out for a meal with her husband. He had decided to treat her in a bid to cheer her up, so they had gone to a beautiful fish restaurant in a small village near where they lived. Paula was very quiet during the meal, not eating very much.

"Is everything okay, honey?" Matt asked.

"Yeah, I'm fine."

"Well, you don't look fine to me. In fact, you look like you don't want to be here. Is it work? Or have I done something wrong?"

"No, it's nothing you've done. You've been great lately. I just don't know what to do at the minute. I hate my job and there's nothing I can do about it. It's all I know."

"And it's just down to this one bloke?"

"Yup. We're just complete opposites. I'm sure he's a lovely bloke when he's outside of work, but inside that surgery he's a complete prat. Not that it matters what I think, because the partners love him. We seem to be in conflict every day."

Matt had heard the story on numerous occasions over the last few weeks, but this time a small bell went off in his head. The word 'conflict' had triggered something in his brain; a recent conversation with someone. He tried to dredge up the memory and recall who he had been speaking with. Then he remembered; he had spoken to a man at a recent networking event. He had told Matt about his business, Conflict Management and Mediation.

"It's got to be worth a go. I hate seeing you like this but I'm sure this Mo chap isn't a total monster. You just need somebody to help you to thrash it out together!" Matt had said the last part of the sentence in a jokey tone, but Paula was not amused.

"Do you think I'm overreacting? That some stranger can just pitch up and, hey presto, we're best friends forever?" She sat back and took a large gulp of wine.

"I just don't see what harm it can do, getting in an expert to try and resolve the issues. It's often best to talk things through with somebody who's detached from the situation. Get some fresh eyes on it. He seemed to know what he was talking about..."

"Okay, okay, I'll mention it to the partners, only so you'll shut up about it."

Paula had assumed that the doctors would have no interest in paying for a mediator to come in to try and resolve the situation between Mo and the rest of the staff. She was shocked when both the partner and Mo agreed that it was a great idea. Therefore, here she was, just three weeks later, sat in the surgery's small meeting room, face to face with a short, bulky, middle-aged man called Brian. She was not convinced he was the answer to her problems.

He started off by explaining that he would be talking to both Paula and Mo individually first. He would assess their willingness to work together to resolve the issue. Then he would get them together, open up communication and explore options for a way forward for them. The aim was to get them working together productively and successfully for the betterment of the surgery. Paula was sceptical.

Twenty-four hours later, Paula found herself walking back into the meeting room. She was greeted by Brian, sat behind a desk, looking eager and ready to begin the day's proceedings. Only this time there was an extra person in the meeting room. Mo Akhtar was sat opposite Brian. He turned his head and greeted Paula with a curt, "Morning", before turning back and looking straight ahead. Paula took the seat next to him and they both faced Brian.

"Right, you're both here because, as you're aware, there have been a few issues between the two of you and the partners here are keen for them to be resolved. Now, the good news is that having spoken to both of you, there is a good possibility that we can get you on the same page and working successfully together."

She had heard similar phrases from the partners, but somehow it sounded more assuring coming from Brian. Maybe it was the fact that he was not part of the practice, or maybe it was just that Paula was in a better frame of mind following her chat with Brian.

"Now, one piece of common ground that was coming through strongly when I spoke to you was that you both want this place to be a success. Paula, you've been here for a long time, enjoy working here and have seen the surgery grow to be a great success. Mo, you've got a fantastic background in management. You've identified some areas where improvements can be made and tried to implement them. Agreed?"

Both Paula and Mo nodded and glanced at each other. Brian smiled and carried on. "You're going to start by listening to what each other has to say about the situation. Mo, I want you to go first. Tell us about yourself, then talk about your job. What do you want to achieve, what do you want for the surgery and what do you think about Paula? Paula, just listen to what Mo has to say. You will have your turn to speak next."

Mo started by talking about his previous jobs. Whilst the information was not especially interesting, Paula was taken by how much sense Mo was making. When he spoke about the surgery, he sounded genuine and sincere. Paula found his speech compelling and heartfelt. He did want the surgery to succeed, but more surprisingly, he spoke of his great desire to help the surgery staff and to get on with them all. Paula was beginning to see Mo in a different light.

The meeting continued with Brian skilfully using other techniques to open up communication and understanding with both of them. Paula could feel herself getting less tense as time went by.

"Now, you may not need to become best friends or even good friends. Remember, this is about ensuring your patients get the best service possible and that you and the rest of the staff are happy at work." More nods in agreement.

"Excellent!" Brian clapped his hands together. "Let's get on with more of this! Next, grab a pen and paper and I want you to both spend ten minutes jotting down what you would like the other person to do differently."

By the end of the day, Paula was feeling a lot more comfortable in Mo's company. She was still convinced they were never going to be friends but thanks to Brian's prompts and the neutral environment, she was at least seeing that he was not the 'enemy'. Indeed, she had to concede that he had some good ideas and knew what he was talking about. She was also pleasantly surprised that Mo had listened closely to her input and even appeared to agree with some of her views. She still found his dress sense, mannerisms and business language annoying, but she was becoming less bothered by these issues. She had not suddenly decided that Mo was a great person and her new friend, but she did believe they could work together at the surgery. And that was progress!

Matt wearily opened his front door. He had been away with work for a week and was feeling extremely tired. He had spent five hours driving and needed some food and drink. As he drove his car into his drive, he was slightly apprehensive about seeing Paula. They had spoken briefly during the week so he was fully expecting his wife to be in the same poor mood that had plagued her in recent times. Therefore, he was somewhat bemused when he was greeted by a massive hug and handed a glass of red wine.

"I have missed you so much!" Paula said, finally releasing him from the hug.

"Good week?" Matt asked.

"Not bad. Now, you sit down and I'll cook dinner. What do you fancy?"

The following day at work, all the staff received a memo from the partners. They wanted volunteers to form a working party to look at ways of improving the waiting time for patients. Paula immediately replied in the affirmative. She was determined to get involved in this project and help the surgery. Following her acceptance, she received an invite to a meeting later that day.

"Great," thought Paula. "A chance to show the partners that I can still be an asset here and I'm over my dispute with Mo."

A few hours later, she found herself walking into the very same meeting room that she had been in a few days earlier. She reflected on how different she felt compared to her first encounter with Brian. There were other members of staff in the room, as well as one of the partners. "Nice of you to join in, Paula," said the doctor. "We're just waiting for one more."

Paula sat down, smiling as she did so. She was looking forward to Mo Akhtar taking up the one remaining seat. The mediator had worked wonders and made that possible.

*****

MORE ON MEDIATION

Here is a summary of the positive outcomes for the surgery as a result of the mediation process.

Valuing Difference – *Imagine what relationships would be like if we all were the same. Quite boring, you will agree! As humans we are all different and it is about **valuing** this difference. Visualise a plate of food where all of it is the same colour and taste. Yuk!*

Now imagine a plate of food with different colours, tastes and textures. Hmmm... tasty. Human differences add spice to life too.

The mediation process with Mo and Paula helped both of them to value each other's differences.

Speed – Mediation can resolve conflict swiftly. Even the most complex case (i.e. group mediation) can be resolved within one to two days, avoiding the lengthy timescales involved in litigation or formal processes which may happen if the conflict is not resolved.

Cost savings – Just think of the time managers spend in dealing with a conflict that has entered a formal process. Imagine the costs to the surgery in the long run if mediation had not taken place. Paula would have probably resigned, resulting in a loss of an experienced, valuable and committed employee. For the surgery, there would be an increase in costs of recruiting and training another person.

Positive working relationships – Can you imagine the staff morale within the surgery if the conflict had been allowed to continue? Mediation fostered ongoing working relationships, allowing Mo and Paula to continue working with each other. A formal/legal process would have rendered this unlikely, and in many cases, impossible. A successful mediation meant there was no loser but a win/win situation and this helped to foster positive working relationships within the whole team.

Mediation is a common way of resolving workplace conflicts. Amongst the most prevalent circumstances that require mediation are:

- **Conflict between peers**
- **Conflict between manager/member of staff**
- **Conflict between senior managers**
- **Group or team mediations**
- **Bullying, harassment and/or discrimination**
- **Conflict between an employee and a third party (e.g. contracted services)**
- **Change resistance (working patterns, work content)**
- **Staff appraisal disputes**

Story 1: The Mediator

Whilst situations such as those above sometimes need third-party interventions, there are plenty of steps that managers can take to help prevent a mediator being required in the first place. Here are the factors that should be addressed to ensure that managers have the skills required to mend working relationships and improve the working environment.

1. **Communication:** No dispute can be resolved without people talking to each other. The more information that managers and employees share with each other, the easier it is to find a solution that works for everyone. This can be helped by managers encouraging employees to open up and be honest.

2. **Leading the way:** If managers set an example by being calm and sensible, then others will follow suit. Problems often develop because people become angry, frustrated and upset. When people feel negative, they are less likely to listen or see any hope of things getting better.

3. **Individual motivations:** Everyone has their own needs, interests and motivations. When a dispute occurs, these traits come to the fore and individuals become entrenched in their way of thinking. Understanding these individual motivations will help managers maximize the varying talent within their team.

4. **Healthy culture:** Managers can develop a preventative culture, rather than a reactive one. Talking openly about workplace conflicts helps employees understand that it is an inevitable element of working life and can help minimize the impact of these conflicts.

Story 2: Never a Waste of Time

1997:

"It must be in here somewhere!" 14-year-old Lee Miller was frantically searching in his pencil case. It was full of set squares, compasses, a calculator, rubber, pencil sharpener and numerous felt tip pens but the one item he needed, a ballpoint pen, was not there.

"Should have found it before the bus started moving." Lee's friend Mark was sitting behind him as usual, and was never backward in coming forward with 'advice'.

"Yes, well I should have done my homework last night, but I was playing my football video game instead!"

Mark laughed. "You know what, mate, you always make me feel better about things. No matter how far behind I am with stuff, I always know you'll be in a worse spot."

"Shut up, Mark!"

2000:

Lee had played *Football Manager* about twenty times but he still loved it. To him, it was the best game in the world. As he got to the end, he seriously considered rewinding to the start and playing it all over again. His parents were out and he had nothing else to do all evening. He glanced at his watch; 7.30pm – maybe he should have something to eat first.

As he walked to the kitchen, he heard the phone ring and dashed to answer it.

"Hello," he blurted, slightly out of breath from racing to get it. It was Lily, a girl he was going on a date with the following night.

"Where are you? Are you still on the bus?" She sounded worried.

"I'm at home, making dinner."

"What! Why are you at home? And why are you making dinner? I'm in Pizza Hut, waiting for you."

Lee was bemused. Clearly Lily had got her dates wrong. "It's tomorrow we're going out." He laughed. "I knew I shouldn't be going out with a blonde."

"I've asked a waiter and our booking is for tonight. You're the one who booked the bloody place. You've done it again, let me down because you can't be bothered to remember when we're meeting up. So, thanks for the sarcasm, but I'm glad I've found out I'm going out with a complete idiot. Oh, sorry, that should be, *was* going out with a complete idiot."

2014:

"If you'd like to come through please, Mr Miller?"

Lee nervously walked into the room and was confronted by three sets of eyes looking sternly at him. He hated interviews and this was for a job he desperately wanted. Shift Manager for a care home was not the most glamorous position, but it was something he really wanted to do. One day he planned to run his own care home, give something back to the community and help people. He had prepared well and despite his nerves, he was feeling confident.

The initial questions were fine: Why did he want the job? What aspects of the role appealed to him? It was material he had prepared for and he reeled off his answers confidently.

"Lee, can you tell me what you know about the Health and Social Care legislation and how that will affect your role?"

Lee felt like somebody had punched him in the stomach. He racked his brains and went through the preparation he had done over the last week. He had covered all the job requirements, researched the company and the industry. The legislation rang a bell, but nothing was coming into his head. "Erm ... I'm sorry, I can't answer that question."

Eyes narrowed and one of the panel members wrote something on his notepad. The rest of the interview was a blur. He had messed up again.

When he got home, he found the job specification and the notes he had made. After a few seconds, he saw it: *Demonstrate a thorough understanding and application of the Health and Social Care legislation*. Why had he not researched that? Then he remembered what had led him to miss it out. He had been going through the job specification before his friend picked him up to go to the cinema. He had lost track of time and was surprised when the doorbell rang. He remembered putting his notes down and leaving. He had forgotten to return to that section.

2017:

"So here I am. Stuck in a boring job, essentially because I've never been good at managing my time."

"It's more common than you think. As you can see, we've got fourteen people in the room today who have the same issue." Jenny Mills, the Time Management Trainer, smiled at Lee.

It had been a big step for Lee to sign up for this course. It was not cheap, it sounded like hard work and he was not looking forward to the home truths that were likely to be coming his way. Ultimately, he had signed up in desperation because the thought of being stuck in a dead-end job for the rest of his life filled him with dread.

His life had been full of missed deadlines, turning up late and being ill-prepared. It had cost him jobs, relationships and qualifications. He knew he needed to address this problem. His manager had expressed concern and threatened to put him on performance management if he continued to miss targets and meetings. He had found the course, '*Time Management – Learn powerful techniques to create and save time effectively*', via a simple online search.

He was pleased with himself for having the courage to sign up. It had started promisingly enough. The venue was a modern little meeting room in an office complex. The other delegates looked pretty normal, as did the trainer. There was even some excellent filter coffee and biscuits on offer.

"First off, we're going to find out about each other. I would like you to turn to the next person and chat for a few minutes to get to know each other a little. Please refer to this example." Jenny pointed at the screen.

IS THIS YOU?

"Excuse me, I have to take this call. I'll be back right after I check my e-mails, see what updates I have on Facebook, LinkedIn and Twitter, decide what to buy for my friend's birthday, check to see if the post has arrived, and listen to the cricket scores. No problem, right? Now, where was I? Oh, yeah and what about that new phone that lets me download my apps faster than ever

and that little online newsfeed in the corner of my computer that's keeping me up to date?"

If this is you, then you are probably into imbalance or HARD TIME which we shall discuss later.

Lee turned to Simone, who was sitting on his left, and after discussing the exercise and hearing her troubles with keeping time, he felt relieved that he was not the only one with this predicament.

When they had finished, Jenny asked everyone to get into pairs for the next exercise of the day.

First, count to 10 as fast as possible. Secondly, recite the alphabet from A to J as quickly as possible. Note the time taken with both separately.

Next, switch between tasks (A1, B2, C3, D4, etc.). Note time taken in seconds.

Reflect and discuss.

Some delegates looked perplexed but all of them attempted the exercise. Lee felt slightly stupid as he went through the task, even more so when he found himself getting letters and numbers in the wrong order and started stumbling.

"It's not as easy as you think," said Jenny. "You've probably discovered that it takes longer when you try to multitask. The brain needs a certain amount of time for *switching*. When you leave one task, then come back to it later, it takes the brain a while to readjust. Those extra seconds add up and when you are constantly switching back and forth, they can add considerably to the amount of time devoted to each task. Bottlenecks are created. This is essentially the same thing that happens to your computer when you have too many windows open at the same time. The time required for switching accumulates to the point that the computer slows down and you have to reboot."

Lee pondered on this. He often found that he had too many things on the go and would agree to do more, regardless of what else he had on his plate. For some reason, he could not say "No".

The rest of this topic covered exercises that examined the workings of the brain and how it was difficult to manage time successfully. Lee found himself agreeing with a lot of the comments Jenny was making.

"Now we're going to look at what type of time manager you are." Jenny handed out a sheet of paper to each of the delegates.

"Have a read through this sheet and circle the descriptions that sound most like you."

TEN TYPES OF TIME MANAGER

1. *The Urgency Addict*
    This individual gets satisfaction from coping with a crisis and always rising to the occasion. There is a lack of planning because they are always firefighting.

2. *The Busy Being Busy Individual*
    This person can make a banquet of the smallest meal and often spends a lot of time telling people how busy they are or how their time is spent, instead of getting the work done.

3. *Trivial Pursuits*
    Spends time on non-important tasks due to a lack of understanding or confidence in tackling important tasks.

4. *The Procrastinator*
    Leaves everything to the last minute and does not complete the task; or needs to spend long hours on preparation instead of getting the task done.

5. *Can't Say "No"*
    Says "Yes" to tasks, regardless of current workload, or their suitability or any interest in those tasks.

6. *Collector*
    Collects other peoples' problems because the problems are related to what they are already doing and they are flattered to be asked.

7. *The Perfectionist*
    Doesn't trust others to do the job as well as themselves or spends all the time trying to achieve a level of perfection unwarranted for the task in hand.

8. *The Over-Creative Type*
    Loses time by overcomplicating the tasks.

9. *Social Secretary*
    Spends time organising social events and talking to everyone.

10. *Over Organised*
    Spends every day planning each detail. Has their diary colour co-ordinated but unwilling to respond to an urgent task or help the team reach its target.

Lee smirked and circled numbers 3 and 4. They described him to a tee. If something could be put off, he would; that was his life. Homework? After a couple of hours playing *FIFA*. Getting ready for a date? After this film. Job interview preparation? When I get back from the pub.

The more he thought about it, the more he became aware that the 'Trivial Pursuits' and 'Procrastinator' descriptions related to him perfectly. Lee began talking to the person sitting to his right, a nervous-looking middle-aged man called Chris who worked in Human Resources and had recently been given a formal warning at work for failing to meet his deadlines. He talked about how he often collected other people's problems and spent too much time and energy on those, to the detriment of his own work. It was a very different problem to Lee's but they both had difficulties in meeting deadlines.

When Jenny asked for feedback and questions, Lee asked, "How do you overcome procrastination? It really bugs me. I intend to do something but just can't find the motivation to do it."

Jenny smiled. "If you have a tendency to procrastinate and avoid big changes, then breaking down a big change into small manageable tasks gets you moving forward. It's called the *Scaling* method. For example, if you want to start eating more healthily but think that swapping from eating take-outs everyday to healthy eating would be too much to achieve all at once, you may want to start by introducing salads into your diet for a week. Step two may be cutting down on take-outs for one or two nights a week and gradually building on this. Next, you may want to experiment with healthy cooking, and so on. By building in the change gradually, you are more likely to achieve and sustain your goals rather than trying to do everything at once. Does that help, Lee?"

"Hmm, yes that makes sense. I've wanted to apply for other jobs and often look at application forms but I keep putting it off, then, nearer to the closing date, I panic. Then it all feels too much so I end up not doing it at all. Then I regret it and get angry at myself. This keeps happening."

"Okay, Lee, so how would you apply the Scaling method to that scenario? We have a scale from nought to ten. You start at nought and sending off the application would be ten on your scale. Let's work on this as a group."

Simone made the first contribution. "Maybe you could start by downloading the application form and saving it as a first step and then just filling in your personal details as a second."

Chris said, "Then just focus on one section at a time, bit by bit, instead of thinking about the whole application."

"That's a great idea," said Lee. "There's a job that I saw on the *Guardian* website yesterday. I might download that today. Tomorrow I'll just fill in my personal details and maybe do another section on Saturday when I have the whole day free. When I think about doing one section at a time, it doesn't feel overwhelming and I think completing each stage would give me a sense of achievement."

When there were no more questions, Jenny said, "I can see you've all circled something, and we've explored some issues that arise from your choices. Now let's look at why you're in the category you've circled. On the back of the sheet is a table where you can outline your weekly activities and how long you spend doing them. I want you to give each task a score of 1 to 4, depending on how well you think you accomplish each task. Working through these exercises will help you to review your activities at work and at home and initiate the process of change that will enable better use of time."

TIME MANAGEMENT QUESTIONNAIRE

'Me-Time' Exercise 1

Analyse how you spend your time

List the main activities you are involved in during a 'typical' week. Try to identify the approximate amount of time you spend on each one, and rate it from 1 to 4.

Activity	Time	Rating 1-4

'Me-Time' Exercise 2

Review Exercise 1 and identify activities which could be left out, thus saving time. Next, list 'me-time' activities which use this saved time more constructively.

Unnecessary activities	Me-time activities

Jenny clicked on the next slide and a lively discussion ensued on time control issues.

You Can Control:

- *Chatting on the phone*
- *Inability to say "No"*
- *Procrastination*
- *Mistakes*
- *Unrealistic time estimates*
- *Mislaying important items*
- *Too much detail*

You Cannot Control:

- *Drop-in visitors*
- *Delayed decisions*
- *Weather*
- *Unnecessary post or e-mails*
- *Misunderstandings*
- *Undefined roles*
- *Overly long meetings*
- *Conflicting priorities*
- *IT problems*

Jenny went on to address the topic of time-wasting by giving the delegates another handout to consider.

TIME WASTING: REVIEW QUESTIONS

Have I 'wasted time'? How much? How?
How much time was given to what I think is important?
How much time did I allocate to my priorities?
How organised was I each day in knowing what I wanted to achieve?
Did anything not 'get done' that I wished had been done because I 'put it off'?
Did I waste other people's time?
Did I set myself deadlines and did I meet them?
Did I ask myself frequently "What is the best use of my time right now?"?
Am I in control of my time or do others control me? Is my time constantly being wasted by interruptions? Why do I allow this?
Is my time planned or unplanned? How much of my time can I really take to plan?
Are there activities that I'm taking too much time to accomplish?
Are there activities I shouldn't be doing at all?
Did I accomplish the things I wanted today?
Could I change the usual sequence of some activities and thus manage time better?
Which of the activities could be delegated to a subordinate, peer, or the boss?

ACTION STEPS:
USING YOUR TIME CONSTRUCTIVELY

Take your top three time-wasters. Now write down 'Action steps' – ways of using your time more effectively.

Be daring! Take a chance!

A.

1.

2.

3.

B.

1.

2.

3.

C.

1.

2.

3.

Lee dutifully filled out his forms, then felt slightly embarrassed as he apprehended his scores. It appeared he was an expert at looking for holidays on the internet, but less adept at ringing up his girlfriend.

Jenny carried on enthusiastically. "Now let's try and identify why your scores are what they are. Are you somebody who is often late? Do you find it hard to juggle multiple tasks? Do you underestimate the time it takes to complete tasks?" Lee and a few other group members nodded along to this.

"How do you treat deadlines? Deadlines have their place. We all have work deadlines, but also outside of work; we have to go out at certain times, we have to have food ready at certain times or have to send a birthday card by a certain date. Daily life is often based around deadlines. We set ourselves deadlines in order to make ourselves think about what to do and when we must do it. Please look at this next list."

DEADLINES: QUESTIONS TO ASK YOURSELF

- *Are you often late?*
- *Do you seem to be juggling several things at once?*
- *Do you underestimate the time needed to do things properly?*
- *Do you enjoy having a lot on your plate?*
- *Do you feel uneasy if a deadline is suddenly postponed?*
- *Do you panic if a new deadline is suddenly imposed?*

After a few minutes, Jenny continued. "But deadlines can also begin to rule your life. If you are always running for deadlines, you may be doing your work or tasks badly. You may be wearing out your body; like a car running at high revs all the time. Some deadlines are self-imposed, some are dictated to you. Some are important, some can be missed without consequences. Some are fixed and some can be moved. So, how should we manage these deadlines?" There was silence in the room.

"If we knew that we wouldn't be here!" Lee thought.

"The answer lies with the **4 Ps**," Jenny said. "Firstly, we need to **plan**. Make a list of your deadlines and when they need to be completed by. Then you can **prioritise** your tasks. Is the deadline short or long term? Is it important? If it isn't, then you don't need to feel pressured into meeting it. If it is unimportant or inappropriate, you can let the deadline **pass** with agreement from stakeholders. Finally, don't **procrastinate**. Keep asking yourself; What is the best use of my time right now? What am I avoiding by procrastinating? Am I frightened of the task or opposed to it? Use the scaling method that we have discussed."

Next, Jenny introduced the **4 Ds of Time Management**. She said that would help create 'Me-Time' to rest, relax and recuperate. She clicked to the relevant slide on the screen.

1. ***DO IT NOW** – important tasks only you can do*
2. ***DELEGATE** – important tasks others can do for you*
3. ***DO IT LATER** – not important or urgent*
4. ***DUMP IT** – no difference whether done or not*

"Taking all of that into account, go back to your 'To Do' list and prioritise your activities. Which are the most important, which can you let pass and which do you need to do first? You can do a similar exercise by listing all your tasks for a week and putting them in the above categories. By delegating and dumping some of the tasks, you make time for self-care and for other higher priority deadlines."

The rest of the morning was spent looking at ways of meeting deadlines and prioritising activities as well as making time to recharge personal energy and enjoy time with loved ones.

Lee felt optimistic and enlightened as the morning session came to an end. Walking up to the room where lunch was being served, he felt like he was getting a handle on his problems at last. Lunchtime was a relaxed affair, as he mingled with the other delegates while enjoying a few sandwiches.

Jenny retreated to some solitude during the lunch break, choosing to sit in her car, away from all the chatter from the delegates. As she ate her sandwich, her thoughts drifted to her own story, which had led to her interest in time management.

Several years ago she had worked from home. As a single parent, she had got used to doing everything for her three young children. This became a fixed pattern and she had carried on doing this when they were all in secondary school. It did not occur to her that her children were becoming adults and could share some of the responsibility of running the house.

The pressure of this and the responsibilities of a leadership role at work nearly led her to a breakdown. Inadvertently, she almost slipped into HARD TIME.

She sought support from a Time Management Coach who helped her to apply the 4 Ds. She made a list of all her weekly jobs: cooking, cleaning, ironing, shopping, work deadlines, caring for her elderly father and so on. Her coach helped her to see that her children were now capable of sharing a lot of these responsibilities and gave her the confidence to delegate.

She went home, sat her children down and drew up a rota for all the household chores. She could save time by dumping her daily shopping and cleaning routine. She started to do a big weekly shop and initiated a joint family cleaning morning with her children on Saturday mornings. Jenny's life turned around after this. She found time to rest and follow some of her own interests as well as meet work commitments. She was less tired and more focused at work. The changes also helped her children become more responsible and independent.

Story 2: Never a Waste of Time

After her own experience of juggling with work and home life, Jenny wanted to help other people live more fulfilling and meaningful lives, so she studied to become a Time Management Trainer.

Amid the usual wisecracks about the quality of the sandwiches and absence of a dessert on the lunch menu, the delegates gathered for the afternoon session.

"This afternoon," Jenny said, once everyone had settled down, "I would like to introduce an alternative approach to considering time management, which is a deeper, reflective way of exploring and balancing the use of time. Personally, this has been life-changing for me and my adult children. We will join in a short relaxation practice and after that, a reflective exercise. Are you all okay to give it a try?" The group nodded in response.

Jenny continued. "Sit comfortably in your chair. You may close your eyes or just lower them if you prefer. Try to focus your attention within yourself. Take a few deep breaths. Breathe in a sense of peace and wellbeing with every inhalation and breathe out the stresses of the day with every exhalation. Do this for a few minutes."

After a short pause, she continued. "Go deeper into the calm space and as you do so, make a decision to view your life objectively. Now reflect on the following questions: Do I allow myself to do the things that delight me? And what does really delight me? Can I allow myself to accept some of the things that I cannot change?"

Lee struggled to keep up with the questions Jenny was posing. He was mystified by the different, unfamiliar slant in the afternoon session. Luckily Jenny paused for everyone to have the chance to contemplate the questions. Lee felt a wave of joy within him as he made a mental list of what delighted him. He conceived it was the simple things like being with his parents and his girlfriend or just having time to play football with the lads. He heard Jenny begin to speak again, noticing that she had quite a soft and soothing voice.

"Now ask yourself: Do I like my work? Do I feel I work too hard or not hard enough? Does my work feed my heart and my soul or have I sold my soul to my company for the monetary reward? Do I need to consider other choices? These questions form the basis of your Outer Life; the world of your outer activities and the various things you do."

Jenny let her words hang in the air for a few minutes whilst the delegates considered her questions. Lee felt more relaxed and was thinking clearly and logically now. He was aware he was not happy in his job and was only there so he could afford the bills. He felt a new inner confidence and resolved to try to find a more meaningful job. In his current one he was dealing with statistics, with no interaction with people and no sense of reward. He needed to do something where he felt he was making a difference to people's lives. This was a new way of looking at his situation and it seemed to be making sense!

"Now we're going to think about your Inner Life. Do you enjoy an inner life? Do you spend time nurturing your heart and soul or on finding out more about the inner you and what you need and love? Or exploring your creative, imaginative self and spiritual self?

"This may be complicated, so I want you to spend fifteen minutes in pairs discussing these issues. Have a think about which dimension of you has more space and time put into it; your Inner or your Outer self? Are you overly goal orientated or too much 'in the now' and have no goals? Is there a good balance between work and relaxation? Do you allow yourself enough time off? I'll come around to see how you're doing."

Lee found the concept hard to grasp at first, however the other person in his discussion group helped him to understand that there was an aspect of 'being' as well as 'doing' and he was more of a 'doer'. Later he was able to talk about how he did not spend time looking after his inner self. He was easily distracted and often wasted time on useless activities rather than concentrating on his own wellbeing. He was beginning to comprehend that now. He had enjoyed the relaxation practice that Jenny recited and made a mental note to search for more of those online.

Over the next hour, there were a few more similar exercises. Then Jenny moved onto the final part of the course.

"Hopefully you've all learnt a lot about yourselves today, so we're going to finish by recapping on some of the topics we've covered. Establish your goals, standards and priorities. The whole reason we want to manage our time better, is to have more of it for the things that really matter. We can start deciding what these things are. Start each day with a 'To Do' list and apply the 4 Ps or 4 Ds. Give it a try. Think about what you need to do for the rest of the week."

Lee considered his upcoming work, his family, his girlfriend and his other commitments. He jotted down the specifics of what he needed to do that week. Then he carefully went over it and decided what had to take priority. He noticed that this still left him with a reasonable amount of spare time. Time for himself to nourish his body; to exercise, relax, contemplate and enhance his wellbeing. This could be useful.

Jenny continued. "Set aside time every week to work on your own growth and development. There are many ways to do this, for example a course at night school, a regular exercise and relaxation routine, time with loved ones or maybe a professional development course. Choose a way that suits you; just make sure you do take the time to work on your own development. Respect the time of others the way you would like them to respect your time. This is the golden rule of time."

Lee thought hard about this. He had not been respectful of other peoples' time. He had been selfish. He had missed dates, been late for work and missed meetings, all because he had been too self-absorbed and not considered other peoples' time. He had to change that and came up with a list of action points in the concluding part of the day.

A few weeks later, Lee was eating his dinner. The phone rang. It was his mother. She called once a week, usually at the most inappropriate moments.

"Hi, son, how's it going? Me and your dad wondered if you fancied visiting us soon? You haven't been over for quite some time."

"Mum, I'm having my dinner now. Can I call you back in an hour's time?"

After dinner, Lee reflected on what he had learnt on his time management course. He had been more disciplined about his time since the course and was now conscious of the importance of family time. He returned his mother's call.

"Of course I can come over. Are you free on Sunday? I thought I could take you and Dad out for Sunday lunch."

There was a long silence before his mother replied. "Err, that would be lovely, Lee. Is everything okay? Are you sure this won't be a waste of time for you? Don't get me wrong, I mean, this isn't something you'd normally do. You always appear to be rushing, busy and under pressure."

Lee laughed. "How can that ever be a waste of my time, Mum? Things have changed a bit. I'll tell you about it when I see you." He chuckled as he put the phone down, noticing the feeling of warmth and love deep within him.

*****

MORE ON TIME MANAGEMENT

We hear the work/life balance debate all the time. For many people, there may be an imbalance between the time and energy they spend at work and that which they spend at home or with the rest of their life.

Do you feel there is enough balance in your life?

Reflect on the following:

Do you live too much of an **outer**, and not enough of an **inner** life, or vice versa?

Do you spend too long at work and not enough time at home?

Or, figuratively speaking, do you spend too long 'meditating and writing commercially unviable poems' and so do not spend enough time earning money for your family?

What are some of the more rewarding and balancing factors in your life?

What are some of the less revitalising and less balancing features about your life?

Here are some signs of imbalance or being in **HARD TIME**:

Your life seems to:

- Be a struggle or an effort
- Be hurried and pressured
- Creates fear and anxiety
- Deny you simple pleasures
- Have something missing
- Make you numb and joyless

You are:

- Lonely, depressed, tired, exhausted
- Wasting time and not enjoying work
- Bored and frustrated
- Losing control of your life
- Losing your sense of humour and perspective
- Thinking what you need to do next, rather than now
- Overly concerned with status, position or appearance

What three things can you do differently to bring more balance and harmony into your life? List them here:

1.

2.

3.

Carry on working on the 4 Ps and the 4 Ds step by step until you are in complete balance or in **SOFT TIME**.

You will know you are in SOFT TIME when your life:

- Makes you happy and fulfilled
- Allows you to live in the moment
- Makes you open-hearted and generous
- Gives you inner peace and harmony
- Makes you lead rather than follow
- Gives you a sense of freedom

And you are:

- Spontaneous and uninhibited
- Enjoying the simple pleasures of life
- Enjoying silence and solitude
- Seeing the bigger picture
- Trusting your own inner wisdom and judgement
- Feeling joy and blissful

Story 3: Built for Resilience

Paul walked back to his desk. It was Friday afternoon, and in just over an hour he would be driving home, looking forward to a few drinks and a Saturday morning round of golf. His thirtieth birthday was just under a month away and he was excited about planning a big night out with his golf friends to celebrate. Paul also had this niggling, unsettled feeling in the pit of his stomach.

His moments of calm and happiness were few and far between but at least he had a few things to look forward to this weekend. He sat at his desk and checked his emails. Friday afternoon was usually a very quiet time for his inbox, so he was surprised to see that he had received two new emails in the five minutes since he had last checked. He considered ignoring them until Monday; after all, what could he possibly do at 3:30pm on a Friday that could not wait until 8:30am on Monday? His curiosity got the better of him and he reluctantly opened the first of his new messages:

"I've decided I don't want to talk to you at the minute. You just end up making me upset. It's both of our faults, but quite frankly I'm better off without you at present. Please don't call me this weekend. Besides, I'm sure you'll be too busy getting drunk and hitting a ball around a field to give a toss about me anyway!
Take care,
Kate x"

Kate had been Paul's girlfriend for five years, they had a house together and for a long time, seemed the perfect couple. But over the last year, the relationship had been strained. Privately, Paul knew that it was largely his fault. He had been fed up with his job at Crest; he had been promoted from the sales team and was now a Sales Team Manager. He had much preferred the cut and thrust of being a salesman; sitting behind a desk all day carrying out admin tasks was not really Paul's thing. Give him a customer and a product and he was well away, but give him ten members of staff and he was not very good at motivating them or organising their working days.

It was not what he expected; Paul had fancied the idea of being a 'people manager', a chance to inspire, to pass on his sales knowledge, plus he would be earning a few more quid! Unfortunately, the role was not what he had been hoping for. The recession was slowing down sales, he missed the art of selling and he found the paperwork mind-numbing. His manager had spoken to him on various occasions about his performance, and at his previous monthly appraisal he had been told that his performance was under review. If this carried on, he would be in line for a formal warning and possibly worse.

As a result, he had been experiencing long spells of unhappiness and had been argumentative. Kate had borne the brunt of Paul's bad moods and their relationship had deteriorated. Three weeks ago she decided she had had enough, packed her bags and moved back in with her mum. Paul had not made much of an effort to stop her because they needed some time apart. Besides, he had actually enjoyed the time he had to himself. He had missed Kate, but her absence had meant more nights out with friends, more sport on the TV and more rounds of golf. He did not want to split up with Kate but he was happy with the current arrangement for a little while longer.

Paul debated whether or not to reply to the message. In the end he resisted the temptation to say something sarcastic and decided to respect her wishes and not communicate with her.

Message two was very odd:

"Paul – top news! We have got spare budget to spend and I thought it'll be great to send you for some coaching. Don't worry, it's not finding out about some boring spreadsheets or learning a new program. As we have discussed in your one-to-ones, you've been finding things tough over the last few months, but I have every faith in your ability.

So, I've decided that you could benefit from some resilience building training. It's in-house and aimed at helping you to perform at your peak despite our high-pressure culture, to feel better about yourself and ultimately be a better manager. I can vouch for the effectiveness of the sessions, and I think you'll find them highly beneficial. You should have an email from the company with full details of content, times, etc. I expect the first session will be in about two weeks.

And don't worry about missing time at your desk; Jen will look after things. We'll brief her next week. I'll also send you a meeting invite soon, so we can discuss this and what I want you to get out of it. Actually I wish I was going myself!
Mal"

Paul slumped back in his chair. He considered his options for getting out of the sessions. Illness? Too obvious, and besides he'd had a week off 'sick' recently. True, he hadn't technically been unwell, but he'd been feeling overwhelmed by the job and decided a few days at home were in order. Holiday? Non-starter – he only had three days left to book for the year and he needed them for Christmas. He racked his brains for some more ideas but could not think of a plausible option. It looked like he was going to have to go.

Paul spent most of his final hour at work and his drive home in a bad mood. He had never understood the point of this type of coaching, whatever you chose to call it, aimed at improving your wellbeing or building resilience. Surely it was just a case of getting a grip and riding out the bad times. He did not need some New Age person telling him what to do. How was that going to improve the sales figures? He found some heavy rock music on his iPod and played it at a high volume for the duration of his drive home.

By the time he got home, Paul had decided on the most suitable course of action for the evening; get drunk and try to forget about his upcoming misery. He had planned to meet his best friend Adam at their local pub that evening but that was not for another two hours. That seemed like an eternity, so he decided to get started early and have some cans of strong ale before going out. He put a ready meal in the microwave, got changed out of his suit and settled down for some time in front of the TV. Paul thought, "A few beers, a lasagne and *Deal or No Deal* are all I need to feel relaxed!"

"All I'm saying is that there is no harm being open-minded about it." Adam put his pint glass on the table and looked at Paul. They had been friends for over fifteen years and Paul felt comfortable talking to Adam about anything going on in his life. Since Kate had moved out, he had found Adam a great help in keeping his spirits up and offloading his problems. Adam was one of those people who seemed to find life easy. He was married, ran his own business and seemed to be going off on holiday at least once every few months. He was a great friend and Paul was comfortable talking to him about anything.

"Okay, I'll admit that things have been a bit stressful lately. I mean, I've lost my girlfriend and I hate my job. Who wouldn't feel stressed out?"

"Yeah, but this is a great chance to sort it out. I just think it's worth a try."

Paul looked unimpressed. "I'm just going through a rough patch. A few beers is all the therapy I need!"

Adam laughed. "If only that were true. A few pints and all your problems go away."

"That's how it works?"

Adam raised an eyebrow. "For a few hours maybe. But wake up tomorrow and you've still got your problems." He pointed at his half-empty pint glass. "This isn't the solution."

"Hmm, that seems a bit hypocritical."

"Not at all. I drink 'cos I enjoy it and it's sociable. It's not 'cos I want to solve anything or forget my problems."

Paul looked at his friend thoughtfully.

"Well, that's lovely, but I've got a load of stuff I want to forget about and this is a great way of doing it. Same again?"

Paul pointed to his glass and got up to go to the bar. As he waited to be served, he thought about Adam's words. He had been drinking a lot lately, largely because he wanted to forget about work, Kate and the moribund state of his life. Still, he was sure it was just a phase and he would be back on track soon enough. *Wish You Were Here* came on the jukebox. It was one of his favourite songs, but it was not what he wanted to hear at that moment.

When he returned to Adam, they chatted about football, music and a film they had both recently watched. For a short while, Paul forgot about his problems and all was well with the world.

The office of Mal Lovell was rarely visited by the employees of Crest. Mal was a well-respected manager and preferred to adopt the 'less is more' approach to running the company. If you were summoned to his office, you knew it had to be something important. Hence, it was with some trepidation that Paul knocked on the door. It was the day before his resilience building training started and Paul was expecting a thorough grilling on what he was expecting to get out of the sessions. Mal did not disappoint him.

"Ah Paul, all set for tomorrow?" Mal was sat behind his desk, arms folded and with a stern look on his face.

"I think so. Just need to do a quick handover."

Mal raised an eyebrow. "That wasn't exactly what I meant, Paul. I was talking about your prep for the trsiining."

"Oh, they haven't sent me any prep work to do."

"And you didn't think to use your initiative, find out more about it and work out what you wanted to get out of it?"

Paul paused. Mel was right but Paul did not like to admit it. "Well, I was going to have a read up tonight and have a think on the drive in tomorrow."

Another raised eyebrow. "Is that so?" Mal unfolded his arms and leant forward.

"Look, Paul, I don't spend money on training like this for nothing. It costs a lot of money and we've got a sales manager out of office during busy periods. These sessions are vital to your future with Crest. We need you performing at your best, as well as happy, calm and motivated."

Paul felt a bead of sweat forming on his forehead. He had barely given the training a second thought over the last few days. The only positive he could see from it was that it was time out of the office. Since he had received the 'invite', he had far more pressing issues to deal with. Kate had not been back in touch, his team's sales figures were reaching new lows, and he had been feeling increasingly despondent. He was finding it hard to sleep. He was having angry outbursts at work, at home and when he was with friends. The last thing he needed now was to listen to some hippy mumbo jumbo.

"I'm sorry, Mal. I've had a lot on lately."

Mal sighed. "That's part of the problem. You're letting it all build up. I can tell just by looking at you. You're not sleeping, you smell of booze and your team are looking unmotivated and bored. You're meant to be inspiring them, not making them want to leave."

Paul felt like a naughty schoolboy. Mal had not raised his voice, but Paul could tell he was not happy. Nonetheless, he could not see what he could do in the next few days to turn things around.

"Okay, I'm sorry. I'll give this my full attention. I'll work hard and I'll get my team's figures up."

"That's what I want to hear. Now make sure you do what you say you're going to do."

As Paul set off the next morning, he had a heavy sense of foreboding; he hated training and this one had a very high chance of not only being boring, but also making him feel extremely uncomfortable. He parked up and made his way to the meeting room that had been designated for the first session.

By the end of the first session, Paul had slightly revised his opinion of Mal's decision to put him forward for the training. It was not life-changing, but he had to admit Jane, the trainer, knew what she was doing and knew how to engage the audience. During the first session, he got to like Jane; she believed in what she was passing on and spoke with passion and humour.

"Resilience is about the ability to bounce back from adversity in the shortest possible time. When you are resilient, you are calm, relaxed, focused, happy, in control, highly effective, making good decisions, energetic, healthy, approachable and cheerful. It is possible to be this way most of the times in our lives, regardless of the challenges we may be facing.

"Every one of us, including you, has the ability within to be resilient, and we can all learn to do so using simple, practical methods. My aim is to ensure you fully understand the concept of resilience and make simple and practical changes that will increase your resilience considerably."

To Paul's surprise, he was finding himself nodding along to Jane's eloquent delivery although he still retained a degree of scepticism about how this was going to improve his life. That scepticism remained until lunchtime, when he decided to take himself off to the park across the road and spend some time on his own. He sat on a bench gazing out at the green space bathed in sunshine, and mentally checked out his resilience levels. His thought train was interrupted by a female voice.

"Mind if I join you?" It was Jane. She was carrying a cup of herbal tea and looked totally relaxed.

"Go for it," Paul replied. "It's a lovely spot."

Jane sat down and for about a minute they sat in silence gazing out at the gorgeous scenery. Eventually, Paul decided the silence was getting awkward.

"I enjoyed this morning. Lots of good stuff."

Jane smiled. "Thank you. I've been doing this job for about eight years and I still love hearing positive feedback."

"Yeah, it's been far more interesting than I expected."

Jane laughed. "Well, listening to me talking isn't going to solve all your problems. If I could do that, I'd be rich, famous and sitting on a beach in Hawaii. Sadly, life's more complicated than that. Often, the biggest step is realising that you can make things better."

"Can I? My girlfriend's left me, I hate my job, I drink too much and I feel unhappy most of the time."

"You probably think I'm making this up to make you feel better, but a friend of mine was in a similar place a few years ago. She worked for a multinational company who did not care about her, she split up with her husband and was smoking heavily."

"And then she had an epiphany and suddenly everything was great?" Paul realised he sounded sarcastic, but this was exactly the type of tale that made him cynical about this type of training.

"No." Jane looked offended. "That doesn't happen. As it goes, she had to work hard to get back on track. She had to take risks and make sacrifices. But you know what? She now does a job she loves, has just got engaged, stopped smoking and has even started writing music."

Paul was impressed by the passion in Jane's voice. Maybe there was a way out of his rut. However, it was her final words that piqued his interest. He had also wanted to be involved in music and loved listening to people talk about their experiences of songwriting and performing.

"Writing music? What sort? Does she play live?"

Jane grinned. "I knew I could make you listen eventually! She used to play in a band, they were fairly big. Folky type stuff. She was the guitarist. Did a few festivals and released a couple of singles. But they split up when they all started getting married and having kids. Now she's in a good place and thought she'd give it another try. I listened to some of her music last week. It's early days, she's getting a few ideas down and coming up with tunes, but it sounds really good."

"Brilliant. I'm a mere sales manager. Always wanted to work in music but my mother was against it. Consider me jealous."

"I don't want you to be jealous. I want you to be inspired."

With that, Jane got up, announced that her tea had gone cold and walked off, leaving Paul feeling a combination of inspired, slightly embarrassed, but oddly happy.

In his next session with Jane after a few days, he noticed he was 'in the zone'. A phrase he liked to use when he was completely focused on something. He had heard athletes refer to being 'in the zone' during races and felt that it applied just as well to his life. Paul felt at ease talking about his problems and frustrations. It felt like a great weight being lifted off his shoulders.

If the initial session was about self-realisation for Paul, then the subsequent ones were about beginning to find solutions and ways forward. Jane's guidance had made him aware that it was not going to be easy, but with some effort he might just be able to get there.

"To be fully resilient, we need to pay attention to all parts of ourselves – physical body, mind, emotions, relationships and life purpose – in equal measure. If you are not doing this then, can you still expect to continue to function at your peak at all times?"

"Hmm," said Paul, "I must have been neglecting most parts of me from what you say."

Later on, Jane explained how to achieve optimum resilience by following the five steps that involved nourishing the physical body, mind and thoughts, emotions, relationships and life purpose.

"Let's now talk about nourishing your physical body."

"That sounds like you want me to eat loads. I can tick that box already."

Jane laughed out loud. "Not exactly. I'm talking about stopping your bad habits. Instead of having a few beers when you get home from work, why don't you try going for a long walk?"

"I don't enjoy long walks."

"Well no, but it's just an example. You could read a self-help book, eat healthily, go for yoga or Pilates, meditate or go to the gym. I'm just saying that there are better ways to nourish your physical body than a few cans of lager. Try a few and you might find yourself thinking more clearly and positively."

When it came to the end of the training, Paul thanked Jane for the sessions and wished her the best for the future.

That Friday night, he met Adam for drinks.

"So how did it all go?"

"I really hate saying this, but you were right."

"You mean you enjoyed it?"

"Yeah, but not just that. It's opened my eyes to where I'm at and what I need to do. Got some useful tips and ideas. I'm actually excited about the future."

Adam made a grand gesture of feeling under the table and looked at Paul's ears.

"Are you wearing a wire?"

"Huh?"

"Well, there are two options here. Either you're an imposter and the real Paul Mason has been kidnapped, or this is some kind of wind up and Jeremy Beadle is about to walk in!"

Paul grinned. "For a start, Jeremy Beadle died a few years ago so that seems unlikely. Secondly, I don't have any rich friends so there wouldn't be much of a ransom if I was kidnapped. Thirdly, I'm being honest. It was great. Really inspired me and made me think."

"Seriously, mate, I'm chuffed for you. So what's made you suddenly feel so positive?"

"Like I said, got loads of tips and ideas. For example, don't laugh, but I've started meditating every day."

Adam did laugh. "Now that I would love to see!"

"It's great. I just spend ten minutes in the morning with my eyes closed focusing on calm images and words. Makes me feel relaxed and ready for the day. Also, whenever something is bothering me, I write it out and don't bottle it up. Works wonders!"

"That's great, Paul. So, what's the plan?"

"Well, the reason I'm a sales manager in an office is because I applied for the job and I was the best person for it, so there's no point getting down about that. After all, I wouldn't have got the role if the bosses didn't think I was up to it. What I need to do is turn the situation to my advantage, do the best job I can and show my boss what I'm made of."

"Brilliant to hear that, mate. And Kate?"

"I've been an idiot. I've been unfair to her and I don't deserve her... But if there's a chance to get her back and make up for everything, then that's what I'll try and do." Paul delivered the words with a steely determination. For the first time in ages, he was feeling positive and clear about what he wanted.

Six months later, Paul once again found himself being summoned to Mal's office. However, this time he did not feel intimidated by the prospect of facing his manager. This time he felt calm and confident.

"Paul, come on in. How's it going?"

"It's going well." Paul was not lying. His sales results for the last quarter had improved considerably, his team had been performing much better and he was up to date with all of his paperwork and admin.

Mal broke into a rare smile.

"That's what I like to hear. A happy worker is a good worker. I've always had faith in you. I'm glad that you've now got faith in you." He looked at the paperwork on his desk. "To be honest, Paul, it's all positive from me. You are meeting all your targets; your staff are happy and you seem to be in a good mood. I'm pleased for you. How's the home life?"

"Fantastic! Kate's moved back in and we've just booked a holiday to Portugal for Christmas."

"Good to hear it! Look, Paul, we need to have a chat soon about a role that's come up at head office. There's a bit of competition out there but I think you would have a chance."

"That's great, I love a challenge. Can you send me the details?"

"Will do. And Paul... keep it up."

Paul walked out and headed back to his desk. He had one new email. To his surprise, it was from Jane.

"Paul, Hope everything is well and you're in a good place. Got a proposition for you. Do you remember my friend who was trying to get back into the music business? Well, it's taking off and she's played a few gigs. Anyway, she's getting some great feedback and has decided to record some tracks and release them.

"The thing is... she needs a manager. It's not a full-time job, but it would be some weekend and evening work. Meetings with producers, bookings, PR, marketing, etc. I know you would be interested. Let me know and I'll pass on your details.
Jane"

Paul's eyes lit up. Life was getting better and better. He believed he was built for resilience after all.

*****

MORE ON RESILIENCE

Paul's story is typical of many people in today's fast-paced society. He experienced a difficult change of role at work. Unfortunately, he did not have sufficient coping mechanisms to manage the situation. He let everything get on top of him, and subsequently his performance at work and happiness at home were adversely affected.

There is a difference between the buzz people get from doing a busy and challenging job and an unreasonable pressure which can harm personal wellbeing. In Paul's case, his circumstances led to unhappiness and arguments. In other cases, it can lead to exhaustion and burnout. This happens when we keep overusing our body, not taking time out to nourish all aspects of it and feeding it with the wrong products.

Paul's situation highlights the importance of being resilient as challenges and adversity are part of life, we all have to face them. But how do we continue to bounce back and perform at our peak levels despite that? Paul's course helped him to do just that by paying attention to all aspects of his being, his human machine.

Imagine a machine. What would happen if you did not maintain all of its parts and fed it the wrong product? It will begin to work less effectively and eventually break down! This is what was happening to Paul.

These are the 5 steps that Paul was helped to follow on his journey to resilience:

Step 1 – He started by attending to his physical body. He cut down harmful products such as excessive alcohol and replaced these with nurturing routines like walking and meditation.

Step 2 – He then addressed his thoughts and the health of his mind by learning the art of positive thinking and the law of attraction, which is about attracting positive outcomes through positive thinking and visualisation.

Highly resilient people have a realistic, optimistic view of the world. They tend to operate from hope of success rather than fear of failure. We all have setbacks in life but it is believing that we can overcome these, that creates positive outcomes.

Think of a challenge that you have faced. What was your belief about it? Did you believe you would overcome it? Was it positive or negative?

For example, if Paul believed that he would never make it as a sales manager and would eventually lose his job, what might have been the consequence of this belief? Jane and Mal helped him to believe that he can be good in his role, which is one of the factors that helped to turn things around for him.

Story 3: Built for Resilience

The following will help you to develop a more positive attitude:

a. *Become more aware of your negative self-talk (e.g. I am no good at this, I am a failure, etc.)*

b. *Get into the habit of thinking with a positive 'can do' attitude*

c. *Always set positive goals – positive thinking leads to positive emotions, positive action and positive outcomes.*

Step 3 – Paul learned to deal with his emotions by writing them out using the therapeutic writing template as below.

I feel frustrated because ......

I feel sad because ......

I feel angry because ......

I feel hurt because ......

I feel positive because ......

I feel happy because ......

Step 4 – He recognised the importance of healthy, fulfilling and supportive relationships and made a commitment to build these with his girlfriend Kate and spend time with his friends who were willing to help.

Do you have a network of people who offer regular practical, psychological and moral support?

Step 5 – What would happen if you had a natural flair and talent in something that was not nurtured, and you were forced to do the opposite? A good example is someone who has a flair and passion for art but has to train and work as an accountant in their family business. Would this person perform at his/her best?

Is your work fulfilling? What do you need to do to be aligned to your true life purpose in order to make life more meaningful?

Paul did this by taking up the opportunity to pursue his music. Live your passion and help others to do the same as Jane did for Paul.

Story 4: No Bullying, Please!

"Good morning. This is the Employment Assistance Programme, the EAP. My name is Laura; how can I help?"

"Erm ... I don't quite understand how all this works. My Occupational Health Officer gave me this number when I went to them with my problems at work."

"Please can I have your name first?"

"Victor."

"Hello, Victor. Are you currently in a private space, where we can speak freely for the next half an hour or so?"

"Yes, that should be okay."

"Great. Firstly, I need to register you on our system and then I can pass you over to a counsellor who can help you."

Laura asked Victor for the relevant information and then passed him on to Rajiv, one of the organisation's counsellors.

"Let me reassure you first," Rajiv said. "Whatever you share with me today is totally confidential. Nothing you say will be passed on to anyone. The only exception to that would be when there is risk to someone; then we might use confidential information to keep you or others safe. For example, if you told me that you were self-harming then we may need to share that with your GP."

"Well, I am not going to harm myself, not yet. That's why I need someone's help, before I get to that stage."

"Good. That's what we're here for, to help resolve problems before they get too difficult."

"So, what I tell you won't go back to my manager?" Victor sounded relieved. "That's the thing I was most worried about. I'm in enough trouble as it is, without that."

"Not unless there is a corporate risk of any kind, then we might have to report the situation."

"What do you mean by that?"

"For example," Rajiv explained, "If you have a company vehicle and you're driving under the influence of alcohol, or you're going to defame your company on social media; situations like that, which put your company at risk."

"I see what you mean," Victor said. "I'm not planning on anything like that."

Story 4: No Bullying, Please!

"Would you like to tell me the reason you called us today?" Rajiv asked.

"I was given this number by Occupational Health. I've been off sick for four months because of my manager. He's made my life hell. I'm starting to get this sick feeling in my stomach, just thinking about it."

"Okay, Victor, just take it nice and easy and tell me all about it."

There was a long pause before Victor continued. "I used to work for another company. I was there for fifteen years and then I was made redundant. I started this job about eighteen months ago. At my old place, it was completely different. If there was an issue, the manager used to sit me down, talk it through with me and I felt I got guidance and support. But here ... but here ... I don't understand why he does this to me ..."

There was another long pause. "Are you alright, Victor?" Rajiv asked.

Victor blew his nose. "Sorry about that. I just can't help getting upset."

"That's perfectly understandable, Victor. Nothing to apologise for."

"So," Victor went on, "I was saying; here it's completely different. I get put down all the time. He expects me to do the job without the right training and keeps piling more and more work onto me. Anyway, one morning, a few months ago, I was walking to the bus stop on my way to work and I'd got so wound up about everything that I actually threw up in the gutter."

"So, the stress was building up for some time and things really came to a head that morning?" Rajiv reflected on what he had heard so far.

"Yes, that's it exactly. Well, as you can guess, I did a U-turn, went home and I haven't been back to work since."

"I'm sorry to hear that. I can see it's been hard for you, Victor. You said at the start that you've been off sick for four months now. Has anything been done about the situation in that time?"

"Well, I tried to sort it out but didn't really know where to start. That's why the Occupational Health lady suggested I call you, but I am not sure what you can do for me."

"I can let you know about other ways you might get the support you need. Tell me a bit more about what's happened since you've been off sick. Have you seen your doctor?"

"Yes, she suggested I take some time off to reflect on the situation but I didn't feel any better after two weeks. Then she prescribed anti-anxiety medication which just made me sleep all the time and upset my stomach, so I stopped that, and then she sent me on a half-day anxiety management course. The breathing techniques I learned there are helping a little, but that's not going to change my manager, is it? Each time I am contacted by anyone from work, I get panicky and go back to square one."

"What has been the nature of the contact from work, Victor?"

"My manager wrote to me to try to arrange a meeting. I said I couldn't go anywhere near work, so we met at a local centre where they have meeting rooms. It was a disaster."

"Why, what happened?"

"He said I have to come back to work and then we can look at how to resolve the situation. His tone was horrible. Almost as if he didn't care what happened to me as long as he had his way, as usual. In a roundabout way, he mentioned dismissal because my performance wasn't up to scratch. That really worried me. I have a mortgage and a family to support. I can't afford to lose my job."

"Thanks, Victor, you're doing great. I know this must be difficult for you, sharing this with me," Rajiv said. "If you want, there are two aspects we can explore that may help you. First, we can look at some general coping strategies that would clear the muddle in your head and hopefully reduce the anxiety. Secondly, we can look at the specific work issues and seek some ways forward. How does that sound to you?"

"Well, I can't carry on like this. I have to do something, so I'll give it a go. I've not had a decent night's sleep for months now."

"I'm going to do my best to help you with that, Victor. On a day-to-day basis is there anything you do that helps to keep you healthy and less stressed?"

"I take my dog for a walk sometimes and that seems to help."

"That's great, Victor. Regular physical activity is good for relieving stress. Maybe you can aim to take the dog out more often. What would you say you do with all this frustration and fear that has built up inside you?"

"Nothing really, I try to shut it out by watching TV or doing odd jobs in the house, but these days I don't even do that. My wife is fed up because I just lie on the couch and can't be bothered to do anything."

"Does that mean you've bottled up all these emotions inside you for all this time? No wonder you're not sleeping and not motivated to do much else. There's one thing I can suggest. You can let it all out by using the therapeutic writing technique. It's quite simple. Tell me what you are feeling now?"

"Actually, I'm feeling quite angry as I am talking and thinking about my manager."

"With this technique, you just write 'I am angry because...' and then let it all flow out. You can do the same for any other emotions, like fear for example."

"That sounds like a good idea, I'll try it. I'll probably come out with some strong words but I can see how that might make me feel better, getting it all out of my system."

"I am glad to hear that. There's another technique that may help, and that's relaxation and meditation. I know you learned a few on your anxiety management course, but there are plenty more that may help you. You can find them on the internet. Take a look on YouTube. They'll help with your anxiety and sleep problems. Do you want to make some notes? That way you'll have a plan to follow at the end of our call."

"Yes, that makes sense. Can you stay on the line for a minute while I find a pencil and paper and write some of this down?"

Rajiv heard Victor leaving the room, returning after a moment and scribbling away for a few minutes before continuing the call.

"I'll try and practise these techniques every day, and I'll tell my wife about it so she can remind me."

"Brilliant, Victor. Don't forget that the events of the past few months will have taken their toll on you so it makes sense to take care of yourself particularly well; healthy food, lots of water, but then I suppose you know all that."

"Yes, I do, but knowing it doesn't mean I don't fall into the trap of lounging about, eating junk food. You're right. I need to think more about taking better care of myself."

"That's good, I'm sure you'll find that will build your strength up. Shall we talk about the work situation now, if you feel ready to move on?"

"Yes, let's do that. Thanks."

"Victor, have you spoken to your senior manager about any of this?"

"No, because it may be that this is all coming down from him. I don't have much to do with him. I've only seen him once and he didn't look very friendly."

"What's the worst thing that can happen, if you make him aware of your difficulties with your line manager?"

"He might take my line manager's side. I suppose there's a chance that he may try and help. The Occupational Health lady said that her report will also go to him, so he is going to know soon anyway."

"How about your Human Resources department? Have you spoken to anyone there? Also, there should be some company policies on bullying or a code of conduct that would give you formal grounds to raise any concerns to your senior manager or Human Resources. You can also ring ACAS, that's the Advisory, Conciliation and Arbitration Service. They can give you further guidance. I can give you their number."

"I'm writing all this down and will consider it all, but I have to admit my first reaction is fear. I'm worried they'll all gang up against me and I'll lose my job."

"It's only natural to have these kinds of fears, after your recent experiences but you know yourself that you have to try to sort this out. There is the provision of six free counselling sessions through this service and I'm happy to arrange these for you if you want. That would give you an opportunity to talk about the related issues that we can't cover on the phone today."

"I've never had counselling before. If my friends find out, they may think I've completely lost it."

"Remember, the service is completely confidential and your friends won't know unless you tell them. The counsellor has been trained to help you overcome your fears and build your confidence, so you feel more able to speak up for yourself."

"My wife did something like that when her sister died and it did help her to come out of her depression. I think she'll understand. I'll discuss it with her and maybe try this for myself."

"Good. I'll refer you and you should hear from the counsellor within two working days. The counsellor will set the sessions up and explain how it all works. Do you have any other questions before we end the call?"

"No, that is everything. Thank you, you've been a great help."

After Victor put the phone down, his mind kept wandering over events of the past eighteen months and the struggles at work. He started to write down some of his feelings, as Rajiv had suggested. He then went for a long brisk walk to calm himself down. Later, when his wife returned from work, he blurted out some of the difficult emotions towards his line manager which the phone call had triggered.

"I can't get it right whatever I do. He always finds a fault. He is all 'nicey-nice' in front of other people but gets nasty when we're on our own, as if he gets pleasure out of seeing me upset. I only got two days training when I started and everything has changed since then, but I'm expected to know what to do. I have to work directly with customers, yet we're not trained in the right processes. How can I do my work that way? It went on for the first year even though I kept saying I needed more training. Just before Christmas, he had the cheek to put me on a performance plan. I'm sorry I've not been sleeping and that I've been disturbing your sleep too. I know it's not been very nice living with me recently. Sorry for losing my temper with you over stupid little things. I'm glad you insisted on me getting help."

Later that week, Victor contacted his Human Resources office and asked for the company policy on bullying and harassment. He also carried out additional research on the internet about bullying, which he printed out for future reference. Victor reflected on what he had read, convinced that his manager's behaviour was not acceptable and that he should not have tolerated it for this long. He then rang the Advisory, Conciliation and Arbitration Service number that Rajiv had given him. Several times during the five minutes he had to wait for his call to be answered, Victor considered hanging up. When an adviser finally answered, he was told that he had several options; he could try to resolve the issue informally with the help of HR and a senior manager, he could take his issues to the union, or he could lodge a formal grievance.

At his next counselling session, Victor explored the implications of these options. He told his counsellor that the idea of a formal grievance against his manager filled him with dread and he would rather leave and find another job. He explained that he didn't feel strong enough to contemplate that option, even with the support of the union. He decided to take one step at a time and try the informal process first.

Three weeks later, Victor received a big brown envelope containing the Occupational Health report. The Occupational Health advisor had recommended mediation between him and his manager.

Victor spoke to his wife. "I'm glad you think I'm looking better and don't seem to be so strung out. I think the brisk walking, therapeutic writing and relaxation techniques that the telephone counsellor at the EAP service recommended are helping. I feel I'm managing to let go of some of the stress and my head definitely feels a lot clearer. Slumping on the couch watching mindless television didn't help. I thought that would make all my troubles go away but it made it worse. I was getting into a downward negative spiral. You just have to get off your butt and do something constructive, don't you? I'm really pleased I phoned the EAP. It took a lot of courage, but I am glad I took that first step because that was the catalyst I needed for the turnaround. Also, I was in two minds about going to see the counsellor, but after three sessions I'm beginning to see how it works. Just talking to somebody who's impartial makes a difference. I feel I can say whatever I want and she's not judging me and nobody will punish me or tell on me. It's been good to get it all off my chest and it's such a relief when someone believes you. I might search more about counselling on the internet. I'm curious about the process and how it works."

He found some information online.

What is Counselling?

(Adapted from BACP.co.uk)

What is therapy/counselling?

Therapy offers you a safe, confidential place to talk about your life and anything that may be confusing, painful or uncomfortable. It allows you to talk with someone who is trained to listen attentively and to help you improve things.

How will it make me feel?

Therapy is a very personal process. Sometimes it is necessary to talk about painful feelings or difficult decisions, so you may go through a period of feeling worse than when you started. However, therapy should enable you to feel better in the long run. If you do experience a period of feeling worse, talk to your therapist about it to ensure you get the best out of your sessions.

Will I feel better straight away?

Usually, it will take a number of counselling sessions before therapy starts to make a difference. However, on rare occasions, a single session may be enough.

Does it work for everybody?

Therapy doesn't work for everybody. It is not a universal cure-all. Because you may be talking about very personal and often painful things, it can sometimes be difficult to keep going. Despite this, it is often worth the effort as you can be helped to work through problems.

Will I be able to have therapy that understands my cultural background?

Therapists come from a wide range of backgrounds and cultures. It should be possible to find an appropriate therapist for your needs. How and where you access therapy will affect how much choice you have when selecting your therapist.

Is all therapy the same?

No. There are different methods and approaches to therapy, and your chosen therapist will be able to talk to you about their particular method or approach.

What types of therapy are there?

There are many different types of therapy available. However, in general, research shows that the relationship with your therapist or counsellor is more important than the method they use. Your choice of type of therapy may be limited depending on where you access it. If you have a preference over the type of therapy, you may choose to seek a private therapist.

A few days after his fourth counselling session, Victor shared his thoughts with his wife. "She asked me to write down, in chronological order, everything negative that my manager has done and said. When I did that, I could see clearly, in black and white that his behaviour isn't acceptable and no one should be treated the way I've been treated by him. She helped me to let go of my fear about raising my concerns with my senior manager. So, I wrote him an email and sent the chronological list to him.

Story 4: No Bullying, Please!

That letter I had this morning was from him. He's asked to see me next week to discuss the situation. I'll show you the letter; he comes across as quite friendly and approachable, not as I thought initially."

After the meeting with his senior manager, Victor told his wife what had happened. "We met at the same venue; the meeting rooms at the local centre. I told him I still felt anxious thinking about entering the work building. He said he had looked at my list then said he wanted to know how the way I had been treated made me feel and how it had affected my work. He listened quietly to everything I said and told me that he understood why I was feeling stressed. He said he had received the Occupational Health report and spoken to my line manager, but my line manager was not agreeing to mediation. He explained the legal duty of care and said he'd be taking that process forward, as I am anxious about my manager doing this. He asked me what I would need to return to work and I said the only way I could do it was to work under another manager and to have the advanced training to be able to deal with customers. He said he had heard my side of the story, would now consider the situation and write to me soon."

Two weeks later, Victor received a letter inviting him for a meeting with Human Resources and the senior manager. At the meeting, he was given the option to move to another branch, although that would mean a much longer daily commute. Victor accepted the offer.

"I'm hugely relieved when I think of never having to work under that manager again," Victor told his wife. "But starting in a new place under a new manager is making me apprehensive. What if he's as bad? I have to get to know my new colleagues and all that additional training and travelling too. It's all so much of a worry."

Victor's wife suggested that he speak to his counsellor about his worries.

"My counsellor made me see that I had an exemplary record with my previous employers," he shared with his wife after his next session. "She told me that now I have the skills to deal with any stress I may encounter and the confidence to speak up if things aren't done in the right way. I can also ring the EAP service again for support. If my senior manager hadn't intervened and helped me, I would have left the company. It would have been their loss of a diligent conscientious employee which I believe I am. Just think about how much it would cost them to recruit someone else and train them from scratch? So, basically, I'm able to step into this new role with my head held high and with a positive attitude. If anyone tries to bully me then I'll stand up for myself and say loud and clear, "No bullying, please!"

*****

MORE ON BULLYING

What is bullying?

Bullying can take the form of persistent negative attacks on an individual's personal and professional performance. These attacks are unpredictable, irrational and often unfairly meted out. There are some obvious bullying behaviours, yet most of the time the behaviours are covert and hidden, subtle and insidious. They gradually wear the person down over a period of time. Bullying can be an isolating experience – what might appear to be normal behaviour from the outside can be terrifying to the bullied.

Examples of overt bullying

- Verbal abuse, such as shouting or swearing at staff or colleagues either in public or private
- Personal insults
- Constantly humiliating or ridiculing others, belittling them in front of others, persistent criticism or sarcasm
- Terror tactics, open aggression, threats, abuse, and obscenities towards targets, shouting and uncontrolled anger triggered by trivial situations
- Persecution through threats and fear, physical attacks
- Making threats or inappropriate comments about career prospects, job security or performance appraisal reports

Examples of covert bullying

- Subjecting targets to excessive supervision, monitoring everything they do and being excessively critical about minor things with malicious intent
- Taking the credit for the other person's work, but never the blame when things go wrong
- Personal insults and name-calling, spreading malicious rumours
- Freezing out, ignoring, excluding and deliberately talking to a third party to isolate another
- Never listening to other's point of view, always cutting across people in conversation
- Overruling an individual's authority without prior warning or proper discussion
- Removing whole areas of work responsibility from a person, reducing their job to routine tasks which are well below their skills and capabilities
- Setting impossible targets and objectives, or changing targets without telling the person
- Deliberately withholding information which the person requires to do their job effectively

How is bullying sometimes excused?

- Abrasiveness
- An attitude problem
- A personality clash
- Autocratic style of management
- Macho management
- Strong management
- Poor interpersonal skills

Story 5: I Hear You; You Hear Me

Parveen Ghilani hated carrying out appraisals. Something always went wrong, and she never felt she could get her point across. Today's meeting had illustrated these problems perfectly. She had been trying to explain to Charles, her youngest member of staff, that he needed to concentrate more and stop making silly clerical errors which were causing serious repercussions for the team. Unfortunately, it had just sounded as if she was telling him off and he had, understandably, become upset. She knew she was struggling to motivate her staff and get results. She knew she lacked confidence in telling people what to do and did not have the skills to manage them in the right way.

Frustrated, Parveen walked back to her office, slammed the door behind her and slumped down on her chair, banging her file on her desk as she did so. This management role was not shaping up as she had hoped. She thought back to when she had been made team manager. She had worked as a social worker for fifteen years and had been excited and proud of her promotion. She had not foreseen that she would find her dream job this difficult.

The early part of her career had been enjoyable and rewarding. She had been able to apply her personal values to satisfy her desire to help people and to make a real difference to their lives. Her thoughts went back to one of her first cases – that of a young teenage mother of two children who she had helped to re-house and provide the support she needed in parenting skills. She had also helped her find a part-time job in a hospital kitchen. Parveen remembered how fulfilled she had felt when she had got home from work that day after seeing the look of relief on her client's face and hearing her words of gratitude.

That had been before the cutbacks in public funding and the changes in organisational structures. Since then, those resources were no longer available. Parveen and her colleagues felt frustrated and powerless as they fought for the time and funding necessary to make positive changes for their clients. They began to feel overwhelmed and dissatisfied with the mounting paperwork and automated processes that were being introduced.

After five years of struggling as a senior social worker, a vacancy for team manager came up in another team. Parveen leapt at the chance. At the interview, she spoke confidently and passionately about the vital work of social care, convincing the interview panel that she was the perfect person for the job.

To her dismay, after a year in her management post, Parveen was discovering that being a social worker and a manager were not the same thing at all. She had the clinical experience necessary to guide her staff but had soon become conscious that she had no management skills at all. Her senior manager told her there was no funding to send her on a management skills course. The best he could offer were online courses on the company intranet that she could do in her own time.

She was convinced that she had to do something to help herself. Last week she had cried in her office after someone from her team had shouted at her in front of another staff member. He had been angry because he could not help his client, who was in desperate need of childcare for her toddler. The funding for nursery places had been cut back yet again and Parveen had told him there was nothing she could do to change that.

As a manager, she felt more stressed than she had ever felt. Of course, the extra money was useful – in fact, it had already been spent. But she wondered time and time again if all the additional pressure was worth her lovely new conservatory extension. These days, when she got home from work, she was exhausted. The wonderful feeling of satisfaction she had felt ten years ago, like the time she had helped that desperate young mother to find housing and employment, was now gone. She wondered what she could do.

She hated online courses but was forced to accept that there was no other option. Her body knotted up with frustration. She picked up her file and thumped it down on the desk with a force that startled her. The office phone let out a piercing shrill at the same time.

"Ohhhh … go away … I don't want to speak to whoever you are!" she heard herself blurt out loudly.

She knew she must calm herself, and so went on to direct her thoughts towards the breathing technique she had learned in her yoga class. She focused her attention on her body and the movement of her breath. After a few minutes, feeling a little more settled, Parveen reached for her computer and logged on to the company intranet.

There were a few courses to choose from: *Communication and Assertiveness Skills, Managing Conflict, Management Skills*. Parveen decided that the first one was what she needed and clicked on the link for more information.

"Seven hours!" she exclaimed. "Where am I going to find seven hours to do this?" She thought she may have to give up that day she had planned to spend with her sister. She glanced at her diary, realising she was already ten minutes late for a safeguarding meeting.

When Saturday came, she asked her husband to take their daughters shopping and to the cinema, so she could make a start on the online course. She had rung her sister and postponed their shopping trip to the new shopping centre in the city. She tried to put her resentment aside and turned on her computer.

The course, she read, was made up of five steps. The first step described the three main communication styles and asked the participant to assess their own style.

Step 1. Communication Styles

Aggressive	Assertive	Passive
Pushy	Responsible	Helpless
Arrogant	Honest	Victim
Offensive	Clear	Moaning
Violent	Accepting	Self-hating
Domineering	Calm	Martyr
Bullying	Effective	Vague
Blaming	Listening	Apologetic
Sarcastic	Firm	Inhibited
Manipulative	Understanding	Waiting
Frustrating		Deferring
POWER OVER	**POWER WITHIN**	**POWERLESS**

Parveen wondered if she communicated in an aggressive, assertive or passive way. She felt she was more passive than aggressive and certainly not assertive. She was aware that she was prone to moaning instead of facing difficult situations and often avoided confrontation. She found herself thinking of an incident when she was about seven years old.

The scene was crystal clear in her mind. She saw herself sitting at the dinner table with her parents and brother. She looked down at her plate on the table and felt nauseous at the prospect of eating the green bean curry upon it.

"I don't like green beans," she mumbled.

"Eat it or stay hungry!" her father shouted.

"Pavi … eat it, my dear," her mother pleaded.

Parveen sensed the fear in her mother's strained, stumbling voice. She sat at the table until everybody had eaten, the green beans lying on her plate, untouched. After her father had left the dining room, Parveen thought about his authoritarian behaviour and how her mother told her to do exactly what he asked, to keep the peace. She had decided then that she never wanted to behave like her father.

Parveen blinked and tried to focus on the computer screen but the scenario with her father played on her mind. After a while, she figured out that in her endeavour not to be like her father, she had become passive and still afraid to assert herself. It was ten years since her father's death. She acknowledged that it was time for her to let go of her fear and to stand up for herself. She wrote this decision down in her notebook and moved on to the second part of the course.

Step 2. The Importance of Listening

Barriers to listening and communication

- *Not paying attention*
- *Pretend listening*
- *Listening but not hearing the meaning*
- *Rehearsing what to say in reply*
- *Interrupting the speaker in mid-sentence*
- *Hearing what is expected*
- *Feeling defensive or expecting an attack*
- *Listening for something to disagree with*
- *Looking for an opportunity to confront*
- *Offering solutions instantly*
- *Dismissing importance*
- *Using jargon*

Non-acceptance

We convey non-acceptance by:

Advising, giving solutions
"Why don't you...if I were you I would..."

Blaming
"You are wrong for..."

Lecturing, informing
"But the facts are..."

Name calling, shaming

"You are stupid..."

Ordering, directing

"You must do this..."

Preaching, moralising

"You ought to..."

Dismissing, withdrawing

"It's not that important..."

Parveen attempted the exercise which asked her to reflect on her listening style. She started to make a list of the instances when she had not felt listened to and the possible reasons for this. Her father certainly had not listened to her. She thought of a friend who often interrupted her flow of conversation and would start to talk about herself instead. Her brother had a habit of dismissing and minimising concerns when she shared these with him.

Parveen carried on reading the next passage on the principles of good listening. She paused, feeling happy within herself at the awareness that her husband was a very good listener.

Step 3. Good Listening

Principles of Good Listening
- *Get into the person's frame of reference*
- *Suspend judgement*
- *Resist distractions*
- *Think before responding*
- *Repeat verbatim*
- *Rephrase message accurately*
- *Identify important theme*
- *Listen and search for the emotion*
- *Identify underlying meaning of the spoken words*

Listening to body language
- *Body posture*
- *Breathing changes*
- *Eye movements*
- *Facial expression*
- *Hand movements*
- *Hesitance*
- *Change in voice tone*

Paraphrasing and reflecting is

- *Mirroring the literal meaning of someone's words by capturing the main points communicated by a brief statement e.g.:*

- *You are saying that................*

- *In other words........................*

- *It sounds as if.........................*

- *It feels as if............................*

Empathy

- *Pity – feeling for*

- *Sympathy – feeling like*

- *Empathy – feeling with*

- *Empathy is when one person steps into the inner world of another person and steps out again, without becoming that person. It means trying to understand the thoughts, emotions, behaviour and personal meanings from the other person's internal frame of reference. For example, the feelings a singer or actor experiences, when they genuinely feel the part they are performing.*

For the first time, Parveen felt she understood the difference between pity, sympathy and empathy. She thought of Charles, her junior administrator with whom the communication had broken down in the appraisal meeting. She pictured herself in his shoes and tried to gauge his perspective on the situation. She appreciated that he was only eighteen, just out of school, in his first job and that the transition from school to a working life may be challenging for him. She also thought that he would probably be anxious about failing his probationary period at work. Parveen made a note that in the next meeting, she would begin by asking him how it felt to be in his first job and listen properly to his response. She would try to show empathy.

She then went on to read what the course had to say about consolidating the listening process, by giving an adequate summary.

Summarising
- *Bring together the thoughts, feelings and meanings*
- *Check out accuracy*
- *Close a theme*
- *Keep it simple, clear and jargon free*

Example:
So, from what I understand, you feel angry when your partner does not help with the chores and it's tiring for you coping with them on your own. Have I understood it right?

Parveen wrote down how she might summarise her conversation with Charles. "So, Charles, from what I gather, it feels hard for you to make the transition from a school to a work routine and despite trying your best, you are anxious about failing your probation period. Have I got this right?" She made a note

113

of how she would practice reflecting, paraphrasing, paying attention to body language, tone of voice, use of vocabulary and summarising. She looked at her watch. Time for a break and some lunch.

Walking down the stairs to her kitchen, she recalled a recent post on Facebook about the importance of eating fruit and vegetables in the colours of the rainbow. She opted for a salad made of tomato, spinach leaves, yellow and orange peppers, which she dressed with olive oil and fresh lemon juice. She put aside some blueberries for a mid-afternoon snack. She chose not to switch on the television, so she could eat and enjoy her lunch mindfully, while pondering on the three steps of the course that she had studied that morning.

After lunch, Parveen made a start on Step 4.

Step 4. Communicating in Difficult Situations

- *Saying no*
- *Giving criticism*
- *Giving bad news*

Consider the 3 Fs
- *Facts*
- *Feelings*
- *Future support/solution*

Effective communication is when the 3 Fs of both parties are conveyed calmly and accurately.

Example:
Maureen is supporting her close friend Kerry, a single mother with two young children. Every other weekend, Maureen helps with childcare. After one of the weekends of helping, Maureen gets a call from Kerry, asking her to come again the following weekend, as she wants to go and visit her mother who is unwell. Maureen's leg is hurting so she was looking forward to a weekend off to rest and have some time to herself, but she offers to help Kerry instead.

On her drive home after looking after Kerry's children, Maureen feels angry because Kerry had not asked how she was feeling or shown any gratitude for her support. Before she phones Kerry on her return home, Maureen considers the 3 Fs.

*"I know it was difficult when you heard of your mother's illness **(fact)** and I'm guessing you felt anxious about her. **(feelings)** Is that so?"*

*After Kerry confirms this, Maureen continues. "As you know, I gave up my weekend to help you even though my leg is hurting **(fact)**. I felt angry **(feelings)** when on your return, you didn't ask how I was or thank me. What do you think we should do?" **(future goal/solution)**.*

Kerry replies that she had been too tired and preoccupied with her mother's illness and completely forgot that Maureen had agreed to help even though her leg was hurting. Kerry apologises and both friends agree that they should feel free to express their feelings without feeling offended in future.

Parveen read the next work-based example, in which she was asked to compose a response and negotiate saying 'no'.

Daisy is working on four large projects at work. She is aware that her other two colleagues, Ben and Nita, have only three small projects. Her manager asks her to take on another large project.

Parveen wrote her response: "It sounds as if your reason for considering me for this fifth project is because I have the most experience (fact). Have I got this right?"

(Listen to manager's response)

"I am also aware that Ben and Nita only have three small projects which makes me feel that this is not fair (feelings). I would consider taking on the fifth project if you take two of my current projects and allocate these to the rest of the team (future solution)."

Parveen added a footnote to this entry: It is possible to bargain and NEGOTIATE a NO.

After a few minutes of reflection, Parveen started to feel more confident in her ability to communicate effectively. She continued to read the next part eagerly.

Giving critical feedback

When you need to give critical feedback, use the "sandwich" approach, where positive feedback precedes and follows negative feedback.

Positive
Negative
Positive

Example: "You are very knowledgeable and full of drive. Recently I have noticed that the quality of your work has gone down although overall, your work has been of very high standard."

Allow the other person to respond.

*Listen attentively to their **facts** and **feelings** about the situation. Negotiate **future support***

"What are your ideas for moving on?"

End with positive feedback.

"I really value your expertise in ..."

Parveen made copious notes on how she would address similar scenarios in her personal and professional life and then moved on enthusiastically to the next example. This was about developing skills in giving bad news.

How to pass on bad news

Try to:
1. *Give the news in person whenever possible*
2. *Ensure employee is accompanied by another person of choice whenever possible*
3. *Greet the employee warmly and stay relaxed during the interview*
4. *Have the meeting where there would be no distractions*
5. *Allow time for the recipient of the bad news to take in the information*
6. *Offer empathy, and explore support needed*
7. *Allow time for the recipient to ask questions*

Example:
The Manager smiles warmly as he welcomes his employee Alan and Linda, the HR representative, invites them to sit down and offers them a drink.

Manager: "Alan, you are aware from the recent communications that the company is being downsized?"

Alan: "Yes, I've seen the emails about the changes that are going on in the company and the cutbacks."

Manager: "Alan, you have been a valued member of our team for ten years and it is difficult for me to say this but one of the decisions of the board is to make some redundancies."

Alan: "Are you trying to say that I'm being made redundant?"

Manager: "Yes, Alan, I am sorry to say that you are one of them. Your unit is being disbanded by the end of the year."

The manager pauses here and gives time for Alan to take this in and respond. Alan looks shocked.

Alan: "Oh dear, I have a mortgage and two children to get through university. This is bad timing."

Manager: "Yes, I completely understand that it will cause financial hardship to you, but we have had no choice as the company has been making losses due to the prolonged recession. Do you have any questions?"

After answering Alan's questions on time frames and how the pay-out is calculated, the manager continues:

"We will offer you as much support as we can by helping you with re-employment skills, CVs, interview skills, etc. Linda is your

designated person who will help you gain the skills you may need to find another job. Is there someone you want to talk to now or be with on your journey home, if needed?"

Alan: "I need to take this in first and then I'll probably call my wife."

Manager, as he hands Alan a piece of paper:

"Here is a resource list that you will find helpful, the Employment Assistance Service that includes counselling and financial advice. You don't need to go back to your unit now – you can end your shift now. Please feel free to come to me if you have any other questions. Linda will stay with you for a while if that would help."

"That is tough," Parveen thought as she considered the example. She wondered if her company would have the resources and structures in place for that kind of scenario and decided to check it out with her Human Resources department.

She felt she needed a break after that. She went down to the kitchen and put the kettle on. She made a cup of tea, and reached out for the blueberries and a digestive biscuit. While enjoying the snacks, she reflected on the possibility of Charles not passing his probationary period. As this had already been extended from six to twelve months and bearing in mind his poor work performance so far, dismissal was one of the likely options. Back in her office, using the redundancy example, she made notes on how the meeting might go, if she had to break this bad news to him.

She went on to read the last step of the course, by now feeling stimulated and tired at the same time.

Step 5. The Whole Communication Process

1. *Listen*
2. *Demonstrate that you understand the other person*
3. *Say what you think and feel calmly*
4. *Say specifically what you want to happen*
5. *Consider the consequences for yourself and others of any joint solutions*

The most important thing is to discover what motivates the member of staff; to empathise with them, find common ground, and help them to address common goals.

How would you communicate in the following situations?

1. *At work, your line manager asks you to work overtime in unreasonable circumstances and you want to be able to say "No" to the request, but feel anxious about your manager's reaction.*

2. *A colleague at work who shares your desk is making racist remarks constantly. This has been bothering you for a while, but you have not done anything about it.*

"Hmm …" Parveen thought as she contemplated the first scenario. "What would be the worst thing that would happen if I said no?" She went on to formulate a response based on what she had read so far. She wrote down, "I understand we are short-staffed and you are doing your best to clear the backlog. I am also aware that you are getting pressurised by your senior manager to do so. Have I got this right?"

(Listen to manager's response)

"I have already worked long hours for the last three weeks. I am the sole carer for my father who is frail and I really need to spend some time with him. So, I would like to explore other options for resolving this situation."

Parveen glanced at her wristwatch and noticed she was running out of time and so quickly moved on to the next examples.

3. *A friend calls you at work and wants to go out that evening. You want to go home and rest after what has been a hectic day. You start off by saying you're tired and want to go home, but your friend keeps pushing until you say "Yes".*

4.   *Your teenage son is always leaving the kitchen in a mess.
     His room is also filthy and despite constant reminders, he
     continues with this behaviour.*

Parveen made notes on the first scenario. "I understand that we've not gone out together for some time and it would be great to catch up. However, it is short notice and I'm tired so wouldn't be good company. Shall we set a date next week? On the day we choose, I can leave work early, so we can make the most of the time we have together."

Parveen looked at her watch again and was conscious that the family would be home at any minute. She would have to consider the other examples later, once the children were in bed. Parveen turned her computer off and put away her notes with a sense of excitement and confidence in her new communication skills. She let out a huge sigh of relief, feeling reassured that she could refer to her notes any time she felt apprehensive about confrontational situations.

She heard the thud of a door opening downstairs and the sound of excited voices.

"Mummy, where are you? I missed you... " her ten-year-old called out running up the stairs.

"I need to make sure I listen to and hear them and that they hear me too." Parveen said, grinning to herself, as she made her way towards her daughter.

*****

MORE ON COMMUNICATION SKILLS

There is so much more to effective communication than grammar, spelling, voicing your opinion or calming your nerves in front of an audience. Effective communication is one of the most crucial skills any of us can learn. It affects everything we do in life; how we relate to our colleagues, in shops, writing emails, talking to friends and family.

Without effective communication, an unresolved issue might result in many more problems, such as stress, anxiety or illness. A person may be forced to leave a much-loved job due to the inability to resolve simple problems through discussion. When a relationship breaks down, without proper communication, the people concerned can hold on to bitterness and resentment for years afterwards.

Communicating effectively is a vital skill, instrumental to success, and therefore it should be introduced at an early age and carried forward to all aspects of work and personal life.

Story 6: Less Stress, More Gain

Steve, Head of Global Services, asked his secretary to link his call to the Head of Human Resources.

"Victoria," he said, when she came on the line, "I've just been speaking to our media coordinator. It's all over the papers. How could we have slipped up on this? One of our employees is being awarded £90,000 for our negligence of duty of care. This needs urgent action before others get on the bandwagon."

At the next senior management meeting, they discussed the 8% rise in sickness absence due to stress and mental health issues. Of these, 3% were long-term sick absences averaging over three months. The company had rising sickness absence costs and that could not be allowed to continue.

Steve instructed Victoria to draw up a strategy to deal with the issues. Victoria's first thoughts were that Steve was more concerned about the compensation claims and sickness pay than the duty of care they owed to their employees. Nonetheless, she acknowledged that whatever his motives were, at least something was being done now.

She thought about the way forward. She would begin by hiring the appropriate Stress Management/Wellbeing Consultant who would understand the needs of their organisation and help to develop bespoke programmes. A strategy to address the underlying causes would need to be developed. There would also be a stress survey across the company, mandatory stress management training for all managers and depending on the results of the survey, appropriate follow-up interventions.

Not long afterwards, Victoria, Steve and Alastair, Head of Health and Safety, had a meeting with Tamsin and Kevin, two consultants from a well-known Corporate Wellbeing Consultancy. It was agreed that Kevin would send anonymous survey questionnaires to all the employees, including middle and senior managers. Tamsin would develop bespoke training that she would deliver to the managers. She would make a start at the Ealington branch of the company, where the statistics showed the highest levels of sickness absence due to stress and anxiety.

A few weeks later, Tamsin walked into the boardroom in Ealington. "Hello, everyone," she greeted the group of managers sitting around the table. As Tamsin was setting up her laptop and projector, several other managers joined the group. She handed out workbooks that delegates could browse through while waiting for the training to start.

"I wish to begin by introducing myself. My name is Tamsin Chatterley. I have been in the Stress Management and Wellbeing business for twenty years during which time I've directed research projects, worked across the country helping companies such as yours in reducing stress and building resilience and have also written books on the subject. I love what I do and am looking forward to working with you all. Before we begin the formal training, it would be good if you can share your name, role, and any experience of personal or organisational stress issues that you feel comfortable to talk about. Anything you share will be within the framework of these ground rules."

She pointed to a list on the screen. "My aim is to make this a safe and contained learning environment."

Delegates introduced themselves and a few shared their experiences. One had two employees who were off sick with stress, another said he had gone through depression after his mother's death the previous year, another talked of a difficult relationship with a staff member who had taken out a grievance against him for bullying, another said he could not sleep, due to worry about his teenage son who was taking drugs. Only two delegates said they felt settled and happy in their lives, with no worries.

"As you can see," Tamsin said, "stress can be due to personal as well as work-related issues. This morning we shall explore the concept of stress and how to deal with it initially for yourselves as individuals. This will give you a deeper understanding of how you can support your staff. First, let's look at the definition of stress."

She pointed to the slide on the screen.

The Health & Safety Executive defines stress as:
"The adverse reaction people have to excessive pressure or other types of demand placed on them. There is a difference between the buzz people get from doing a busy and challenging job and an unreasonable pressure, which can harm health."

"We need some stress in our lives to drive us and use up our intrinsic creative energy. We can experience the same symptoms when we don't have enough to do. At the same time having demands that exceed our personal energy and resources is harmful. We need to strive to keep a balance with the personal resources and demands on us, so that we are not in underload or overload," Tamsin explained.

She invited the group to talk about whether they were in underload or overload and the indicators for both.

"Next," Tamsin said, "I'd like you to get into groups of three and work on the exercise on the screen. Write down your thoughts please."

Exercise: What are the short and long-term symptoms of stress?

Some of the symptoms that came up within the groups were: sleeplessness, anger outbursts, lack of motivation, withdrawal from loved ones, irritability, feeling out of control, feeling ill, crying for no reason and lack of concentration and focus.

"Now that you have an insight into your levels of stress and your indicators for these, let's talk about what you can do about it and how you can stay in balance." Tamsin continued. "So, what do you do to deal with your stress?"

Tamsin divided the responses from the group into two tables on the screen.

Things to try	Things to avoid
• Physical exercise • Hobbies • Meditation • Relaxation practice • Writing down feelings so they do not build up inside you • Spending time in nature • Music • Spending time with friends and family • Holidays • Having a break • Yoga/tai chi etc. • Sharing problems with people you trust • Healthy food • Drinking lots of water	• Alcohol • Cigarettes • Recreational drugs • Comfort eating • Processed foods with high level of additives • Sugary foods • Taking stress out on loved ones or colleagues • Bottling up issues and not getting help

Tamsin encouraged each participant to reflect on how they would make changes to healthier ways of reducing their stress. An interesting debate followed.

One manager said, "But I like having a few glasses of wine after a stressful day. It helps me to sleep."

Another argued, "Yes, but you can use relaxation or meditation practice which is healthy and equally effective. At least it doesn't damage your liver like the wine does. Also, there's a danger drinking could become an addiction, which would cause you even more stress!"

The debate moved on to the way characters in television dramas were seen to deal with stress.

"They always reach for a drink," someone said. "Do you ever see a character go into another room and start breathing and relaxation exercises or put on their coat to go for a brisk walk?"

"Maybe someone should try to influence some changes in the way television portrays ways of dealing with difficult situations," someone else suggested.

"But those dramas are just reflecting how most people behave," another argued. "It's not their job to preach!"

It was midday by this time. Tamsin said, "Thank you, everyone. We're going to take a lunch break now. I'll see you all back here in an hour."

"This morning was about the individual aspects of stress," Tamsin said, once they had reconvened after lunch. "We're now moving on to the corporate aspects. These are very important in your role as managers. To start with, let us look at how you can identify stress in your team." She pointed to the screen.

1. *By keeping your eyes and ears open for the indicators.*
2. *From information you receive from others in the organisation.*
3. *From data and statistics that give you an indication that something is not right.*

"Have a chat with the person next to you and share some examples." Again, there was plenty of lively chatter.

"I have an employee who is highly strung and chaotic."

"In a meeting I had last week, a colleague was concerned about one of my team members. He said he didn't appear to be himself lately."

"I have an employee based in Ruminton, whom I manage remotely. His targets have been slipping for the past three months."

"In accordance with the legal duty of care in the Health and Safety legislation, you are required to take action," Tamsin reminded them. "You must see the employee to make an assessment using the management standards and draw an action plan to address whatever is causing that stressful situation. We'll use this afternoon to learn and practice that process. I'll also be writing some guidance notes for managers that you can read on your company intranet."

She referred to the next slide.

Stress and the Law:
Under the Health and Safety at Work Act 1974 and the Management of Health and Safety at Work Regulations 1999, in the UK employers have a general duty to ensure, so far as is reasonably practicable, the health, safety and welfare of their employees at work. This includes taking steps to make sure they do not suffer STRESS-RELATED illnesses as a result of their work.

Similarly, all employees have a responsibility for the health, safety and welfare of themselves and others while at work.

Under Civil Law, employers owe a duty of care to their employee, which extends to their mental health.

Tamsin cited examples of case law which illustrated negligence of the duty of care, where large sums had been paid out by companies in compensation.

She talked about Stress Risk Assessments and how these could be carried out through formal surveys or informally through existing structures, such as professional development reviews and team meetings.

She moved on to the next slide and asked the delegates to get into their small groups for this task.

5 Steps to the Risk Assessment Procedure:

- *Identify the hazards/stress (using audit tools, supervision, observation etc.)*
- *Decide who may be harmed and how*
- *Evaluate the risk associated with hazard*
- *Decide strategies to reduce stress*
- *Monitor, review and assess*

Exercise: To what extent have you been applying your legal duty to address stress/mental health issues in your workplace?

Tamsin listened to the large group discussion that followed the exercise.

"I have this highly-strung employee who upsets everyone in the team and I've never thought to do anything about it. The other day he shouted at another team member, then calmed down and carried on with his job. I thought, that's the way he is and the other team member didn't complain. He's been like this for the past seven years since he's been in my team. I should talk to him, assess the underlying issues and take some action to help him to minimise the impact on the team," said one manager.

"I should do the same in the situation where my colleague raised concern about my remote employee," said another manager.

"Let's look at the kind of issues that you would address during your meeting with an employee. Please refer to the management standards which are on page 9 of your workbook," Tamsin instructed.

THE HSE RISK FACTOR CATEGORIES AND MANAGEMENT STANDARDS

The Health and Safety Executive (HSE) have identified six broad categories of risk factors for work-related stress. These are briefly set out below:

Risk	Issues to Consider
Demands	• Work overload/underload • Physical environment: noise, vibration, temperature, ventilation, humidity, lighting, hygiene • Exposure to potential violence and aggression • Lone working • Night work
Control	• Employee opportunities to: • Participate in decision-making • Influence how work is done
Relationships (Consider job/ task relationships and personal relationships)	• Bullying and harassment • Verbal abuse • Insubordination • Victimisation, humiliation or ridicule • Libel, slander or malicious gossip • Spying, pestering or other inappropriate intrusive questioning (personal or domestic life) • Setting impossible/arbitrary objectives/deadlines • Excessive supervision • Unjustified fault finding • Withholding information and exclusion from meetings which the employee has a reasonable expectation of attending

	• Refusing without reasonable cause, reasonable requests for leave or training, or maliciously preventing career development
Change	• Lack of good, open communication • Significant change • New technology • Competition and changing market conditions • Restructuring • Downsizing • Adopting entirely new ways of working • Stop-start one-off events • Subtle, frequent changes
Role	• Role conflict: conflicting job demands or doing things that the employee feels are not part of their job • Role ambiguity: an employee not having a clear picture of their objectives, the scope and responsibilities of their job, or their co-workers' expectations of them
Support/training/ individual factors	• Staff supported emotionally and practically • Competent staff • Training to obtain necessary skills • Skills/training for new work

	• Recruitment skills matching for work demands • Induction • Constructive advice when things go wrong • Team make up, individual difference

Exercise: Discuss the stressors in your organisation under these six categories

Work related	Personal
• Excessive workloads	• Bereavement
• Training/resources	• Ill health
• Remote working	• Family issues
• Isolation	• Moving house
• Bullying	• Financial issues
• Multiple roles	• Burn out

The room was noisy with the delegates' voices as they assimilated the management standards information.

Tamsin answered questions and then said, "Let's make a list of all the actions you can take as managers, to apply your legal duty of care to support your individual team members. Some issues will be work related and some personal. There are some examples in this table."

Work related	Personal
• Review workloads • Make reasonable adjustments to workload • Flexible hours • Training and coaching • Buddy system • Refer to relevant company policies and procedures	• Signpost to doctor • Pass on employment assistant programme phone number • Occupational Health referral • Company intranet for wellbeing resources

During the coffee break, Tamsin tuned in to the conversation in the room. Some people were still feeling nervous about the insight they had gained on the course so far, while others clearly felt enlightened and excited about improving team effectiveness and relations as well as their confidence as managers in tackling stress issues.

"The last stage today is to apply your learning to case studies, which are in your workbook on page 19. Use the action planning form on page 21, which you can modify. We'll work in three groups with each working on one case study. We'll feedback in twenty minutes," Tamsin said.

STRESS RISK ACTION PLANNING FORM

Name:		Personal Number:	
Unit/Department:		Current Role:	
Manager's Name:		Date Completed:	
Reasons for Plan:			
Summary of Actions Agreed:			
Specific Actions Undertaken by Individual:			
Actions:		**Date By/When:**	
Supporting Actions Required by Manager:			
Actions:		**Date By/ When:**	
Supporting Actions Required by Others:			

Agreed Date for Review:

……………..

Signed by Individual:

……………..

Signed by Manager:

……………..

Case Studies

1. *Jules (23) has been in your team for three months. He is located in another part of the country and you are managing him remotely. You receive his attendance records which show that he is consistently late and has not turned up occasionally without giving a reason. You have a telephone meeting with him and it transpires that Jules uses recreational drugs and that he has difficulty getting up in the mornings after having indulged in these the night before. He has tried, without success, to kick the habit since university.*

2. *Conrad (47) has been with the team for four years. He is known as the comedian of the team, witty and always ready with a joke. For the past two months, however, he seems withdrawn and has lost his wit. In fact, he has been avoiding team members and keeping to himself. You meet with him and ask if things are going well for him. Conrad breaks down and says that his dad died suddenly two months ago and his mother is struggling with the loss. In addition, his wife has been diagnosed with a serious illness last month. He went off sick for a week, two months ago.*

3. *Aataria (30) has been a good hard-working employee for the past two years, always ready to go that extra mile and help colleagues. A team member commented to you recently that she has been snapping at him a few times when he has tried to discuss work with her. Also, her*

appearance is not as immaculate as before. Aataria had a month off on sickness leave six months ago and was friendly on her return for a few weeks but soon became irritated with her colleagues again. You have a meeting with her away from the team in a quiet room upstairs. First, Aataria says everything is fine but when probed further, says that the work is getting too much for her. She says you and her colleagues keep adding on to her tasks, some of which she is not trained to do. She gave an example of a colleague asking her to do his weekly statistics when that was not her role. She said she knew she was a walkover but does not know how to say "No" and worries about upsetting her colleagues and losing her job if she cannot keep up, or if she says "No".

The groups discussed the action plan that they would put in place and returned to the boardroom to give their feedback. As each group delivered their response, Tamsin made notes on the screen.

Case study 1

- *Advise that Jules sees his GP for specialist support for his substance misuse.*
- *Refer him to the company counselling service.*
- *Tell him you will seek advice from HR about the impact of this on his probationary period if there is no improvement in his attendance.*
- *Say that you will be reviewing his attendance each month.*
- *Set another meeting in three months to review the plan.*

Case study 2

- *Refer Conrad to the company counselling service.*
- *Advise him to see his doctor.*
- *Introduce flexible hours so Conrad can contribute to the care of his mother and wife.*
- *Agree to meet each month to review his situation.*

Case study 3

- *Set up a meeting to review Aataria's workload.*
- *Identify her training needs.*
- *Contact training department and send her on an assertiveness course.*
- *Refer her to the company counselling service.*
- *Send a memo to the team asking them not to delegate inappropriate work to Aataria.*
- *Invite her to come and talk to you if she has issues with any colleagues.*
- *Set another formal meeting in a month to review the plan.*

"In addition to the above," Tamsin said, "you can ask for advice in these situations from your Human Resources team, Occupational Health and other managerial colleagues. Don't feel that it's just up to you to resolve these situations; remember to use all the resources available to you within the company. You can make a list of the policies and procedures in your organisation that will support you in reducing stress. I'll be writing some guidance on what employees and managers can do in stressful situations and I'm also reviewing the company stress and wellbeing policy. All this information will be on the company intranet soon.

"Right, we only have ten minutes left, so I would like to hear your experience of the day. As this is the pilot programme, your feedback will be taken into particular consideration. All managers on this site and all sites in the UK will be undergoing this training in the next few months. I'll look forward to your feedback on the evaluation forms. It's been a great pleasure working with you all today. I know some of you have travelled quite a distance, so have a safe journey home and thank you for all your contributions."

Victoria called Tamsin the next day. "How did it go?" she asked.

"Very well, I would say. Out of twelve delegates, ten said it was excellent and did not suggest any changes. One said it was good but asked to cut down on the content as it was too much to take in on one day. Another said the company should not stress us in the first place so we wouldn't need any of this training! I always get one or two who are sceptical of the whole issue." Tamsin laughed. "I've emailed the evaluations to you this morning."

"Great, I'll pass that onto Steve. I can't see why he would not want to champion this throughout the organisation. Hopefully this will persuade him when he can see that there is more gain for the organisation when there is less stress."

*****

MORE ON CORPORATE STRESS

It is worth reflecting on the following as an employee and manager:

What are the costs of stress to your:
- customers?
- team?
- organisation?

Do you have a stress policy?

Are you aware of your standards in managing stress?

Are you aware of your competencies to manage stress in your team/organisation?

Would you know what to do to meet your legal obligations in addressing stress within your team/organisation?

Story 7: To Change or not to Change?

The word change is often used in popular culture. There are numerous well-known phrases that include the word and plenty of famous songs referring to change. It is usually seen as being a positive event; 'a change will do you good', 'a change is as good as a rest' and so on.

Mike Collins reflected on this as he sat in his living room gazing absently at whatever soap opera his mother happened to be watching. His opinion of change certainly was not positive. Three months ago, he had been a team manager at Grafton Market Research Agency. He oversaw a team of ten people, whose job was to ring up the public and ask those vital questions such as what newspaper they read, who they would vote for in a General Election and how many hours of TV they watched every week.

Mike thought it was a pretty good job. He enjoyed preparing reports for Grafton's Head Office, as well as supervising his staff. They were a combination of students and long-term workers – and the team was successful. That was until Jill turned up from Head Office one day.

There were two teams in the office, performing similar roles. As well as Mike, there was another team manager, Lisa, who looked after a similar team. Mike and Lisa got on well and had a strong working relationship. In fact, they had just been for a lunchtime drink to discuss staff turnover, when they walked into the office to be greeted by Jill.

"Come through," she said, pointing to a nearby meeting room. "There's something we need to discuss."

Jill explained that due to budget cuts and new management, they were relocating the offices thirty-five miles away and letting go of the short-term members of staff. The new office would only have fifteen market researchers. This meant that both Mike and Lisa's roles would be altered. Previously, they were asking experienced team members to carry out tasks such as compliance checks and complaint handling. Now, they would have to do it all themselves. Even worse, they were being asked to fill in on the phones during busy periods.

Mike's story

Since that fateful meeting, Mike had grown disillusioned with Grafton. They were messing his life around. He had worked hard to get where he was, and he did not want the upheaval. He was worried that he would not be able to cope with the new role. He had never worked in a call centre. What if he was not as good as the people he was managing? Plus, there was the additional travel and the fact that the new office was in the middle of nowhere. Mike was not happy!

He had assumed that his mother would be understanding and help him through the change. However, her view was that Mike should just get on with it. Arguments became the norm and they both withdrew from each other. Hence, why Mike now found himself sat in front of the TV pondering the merits of change, worrying about his job and dreading the fact that it was just two days to go until the move happened. Earlier mornings, menial jobs and a load of disinterested workers.

"I need a smoke," he muttered, before trotting off to the kitchen and rolling himself a joint.

"That's right!" his mother shouted after him. "Have a spliff, that'll solve everything. If you have enough then all your problems will just go away!"

Mike used to enjoy his mother's sarcastic comments, but now they annoyed him. He took a drag. It was disgusting and he screwed up his face, took a deep breath and exhaled. He was not entirely sure when he had made the change from drinking for pleasure to taking drugs out of necessity. It had probably coincided with his insomnia. He squeezed his fist tightly and slammed it on the table.

"It's this sodding move. Life was great until that point." He took another drag. In the absence of any other solutions, this would have to do.

As expected, the move went terribly for Mike. He had not fully comprehended how much longer his drive to work would be. He had to get up an hour earlier every day.

"Doesn't matter, you don't sleep much anyway," his mother said, completely missing the point.

The extra travel was not the main problem though. Mike found his new tasks unbearable. He was spending large chunks of his time conducting surveys, something he loathed and found utterly demeaning. On top of that, his new team consisted of young, intelligent, postgraduates looking for some easy money before getting a 'proper job'. None of them were going to be there for longer than a year but they all thought they had better ideas on how to run things. Mike was being bombarded with ideas on how to make the office more efficient. He was not interested; he just wanted to get through the day, go home, have a smoke and forget about how miserable his job was.

It got worse when Brad, one of the graduates, sent him an email suggesting a new way of putting together the staff rota. There had been a few moans from staff that the current system was unfair. Complaints ranged from "I've got to work late on Friday, two weeks in a row," or "I need to start later on Wednesday 'cos I need to take my Nan shopping."

As it turned out, Brad's suggestion for making it fair was a very clever and fair one. However, Mike was in no mood to accept that some scruffy student was more intelligent than him, so he just declined the idea and told Brad that it would not work.

At that week's team meeting, it became clear that Brad's suggestion had made its way around the entire office. Mike was subjected to a flurry of questions about the new system and more specifically, why he was opposed to it. Mike found himself spouting off several increasingly absurd excuses for not changing the rota. After Mike had made a childish comment about there being a spelling mistake in Brad's email, three team members got up and walked out of the meeting.

"Where are you going?" Mike asked.

The reply came from Chloe, a usually shy and reserved girl. "I'm sorry, but I've got a job to do. This is just silly. We're wasting time and not getting anywhere." With that she calmly walked out of the room, taking the other two workers with her.

All eyes turned to Mike; he felt suitably embarrassed and defeated. There was no fight or desire left in him. "Err, let's just call it a day, shall we? We can pick up next time. Back to work, everyone."

After four months of this misery, Jill arrived at the office for a meeting with Mike. Mike had been anxious about this moment. He was fully aware that he had been late submitting reports, his call stats were poor and he had had more staff absences. He was fully expecting a dressing down, but not quite to the extent that Jill gave him.

"It's unacceptable, we need to address this situation," Jill said calmly, but with a stern look on her face. "I've suggested that you needed to have some help, but you haven't responded. I've had three separate emails in the last week from members of your team complaining that you've been rude to them. Also, that you've been leaving early and not managing the team fairly."

Mike squirmed in his seat. "Sorry, it won't happen again, just a few teething problems."

"I anticipated there would be some teething problems. One complaint from a member of staff could be unfortunate, but three?!" The tone of her voice was harder. Mike felt a tremor through his body.

Jill continued. "As you haven't been interested in taking my advice, I've decided to move over here for a few weeks. We'll need to work together in addressing your issues. I'm going to oversee things, take the pressure off you a little and monitor your performance. There needs to be changes. I know you didn't like us moving offices, but there's nothing we can do about that."

Mike slumped back in his seat. So this is what it feels like to hit rock bottom!

Lisa's story

"Come through," Jill said, pointing to a nearby meeting room. "There's something we need to discuss."

Lisa Grant and her colleague Mike followed Jill to the meeting room, where Jill proceeded to tell them that their jobs would be changing dramatically. As Lisa digested the news, the prospect of change made her nervous and fearful. What if she could not cope with the role? What if she ended up managing a load of disinterested students looking to do as little as possible? And she certainly was not looking forward to the extra travelling.

Lisa was relatively new to her role. She had been promoted from an agent six months previously. She loved managing a team. She had ambitions of going higher in the company and even running her own business one day. This news was putting a huge question mark over her plan. It was going to be far harder to move up the corporate ladder now that her responsibilities were going to dwindle.

On her way home, she stopped at her local library to return her books that were approaching their due date. Lisa had always been open-minded about life, so she decided to have a look in the self-help section to see if she could find any books that would help with her current situation. After a few minutes, her eyes fell on one entitled *How to Cope with Change*. The author had a name that Lisa could not begin to try and pronounce but the title was interesting.

For the next few evenings, she worked her way through the book, making notes and discussing some of the themes with her boyfriend. After finishing the book, she felt more confident about the upcoming change and had some ideas that she wanted to put into practice.

To try and calm her nerves, she went for long walks and continued to discuss the matter in-depth with her boyfriend. They agreed to make changes to their daily routine. He would get the bus to work so she could have the car and save time. In return she would pick their son up from school twice a week when she could leave work early.

As suggested in the book, Lisa put her concerns into two lists: things she had control over and ones she did not. Lisa arranged regular meetings with Jill, to explore her concerns and areas where she could gain more control. Jill was impressed by Lisa's honesty. The one-to-one meetings helped Lisa to identify her training needs for the new role. She planned to prepare and learn the skills needed. She decided to keep an open mind and ask for help in the areas she found challenging. Finally, she made a point of making a visit to the new office prior to the move which helped her to plan the journey and familiarise herself with the new surroundings.

Story 7: To Change or not to Change?

The new premises were more spacious, had excellent new equipment, air conditioning, as well as a huge garden centre and café at the end of the road. She was confident that she could cope with the change in location, but it was the change in role that was going to be more challenging. Initially following the relocation, it was not easy for Lisa. She found it difficult to adapt to the new work schedule and her new team. To cope with this, she would take short breaks to practice the relaxation techniques she had picked up from the book. These were a great help and she found she had the mental strength to persevere and settle into the new role.

The extra travel was a shock to her system and was proving to be tiring. By the end of the week, she felt overwhelmed, so she met up with friends to talk through her problems. She joined a yoga class for one evening to help ease her tiredness.

After four months, Lisa had settled into the new role and was feeling a lot happier about her job. Her performance had not only returned to its pre-move levels, but she was also exceeding Jill's expectations.

At the end of the quarter, Jill asked to see her in the meeting room. Lisa was apprehensive when Jill visited, yet on this occasion she felt confident. She had far exceeded her targets for the month, her staff were performing well and she had grown to enjoy conducting her own surveys. With that in mind, she was perplexed by Jill's opening words.

"I'm afraid things haven't quite gone to plan since we've moved offices, Lisa."

"Oh, how do you mean?" Lisa asked.

"We're going to have a rejig. Unfortunately, Mike has been struggling since the move, so I'm going to be moving over here for a while, to keep an eye on things."

Lisa felt nervous. She knew that Mike had been struggling but the way Jill was talking seemed to indicate that she was not happy with how the whole office was working. Jill noticed the frown on Lisa's face.

"Don't worry. I'm absolutely delighted with how you are getting on. In fact, I want you to take on some of Mike's work, particularly the management side of things. Do more appraisals, run meetings, look at new ideas and so on. It's a great chance for you to learn new skills. I can see you stepping up a level in the future."

"Wow." Lisa was taken aback. In truth, she was uncomfortable with receiving praise, but this was music to her ears.

"And there's more." Jill reached down into her bag and pulled out a colourful envelope. "We've had four separate emails into Head Office from members of your team praising you." She passed the envelope to Lisa. "Oh, and there's a little something extra in here as well."

Story 7: To Change or not to Change?

To Lisa's amazement, she had won the company's Top Performer award, which rewarded her with a sizeable bonus. Instead of spending her two weeks' annual leave pottering around the Cotswolds, she could now look forward to sunning herself in the Algarve. Now that was a change she was certainly looking forward to!

*****

MORE ON CHANGE MANAGEMENT

This story highlights how Mike and Lisa approached and reacted differently to change. Mike reacted negatively and failed to adapt to his new work pattern. Lisa, whilst at first apprehensive, tackled the situation positively which resulted in a great outcome.

For a few moments, imagine what the world would be like if nothing ever changed. Hopefully you will see that change is a normal part of life as most things do not remain constant. Change is inevitable; it is how you deal with it that is vital to your happiness and success.

Think of a change that you have faced in life, what was your approach to it? Was it one of the following?

- **Resistance** – *refuse to accept it, try and change it back to how it was before.*
- **Survival** – *accept it to a point and put up with it.*
- **Growth** – *accept it, adapt to it, and enable positive outcomes.*

Lisa's approach was the third one. She grew from the opportunity that the change provided. She did this by applying the 4 Cs from her Change Management book.

Story 7: To Change or not to Change?

These are:

1. **Commitment:** This is about 'committing' to the change and dealing with it step by step. Mike was fearful, saw the change as a threat, and shied away from it. He did not face the change; he avoided it and remained in denial.

2. **Challenge:** Approach every change as an opportunity for growth, not as a danger or bad omen. Change is an opportunity to learn new life skills and grow stronger as a person. Lisa learned many new skills that led to a promotion and increase in confidence.

3. **Control:** Change has aspects that we can control and others we have no control over.

Think of a current or forthcoming change and make two lists of all the issues and tasks of what you have control of and others that you do not. Now, work with each issue in the 'cannot control' list and explore possible solutions with the help of your support network.
Lisa did that with her boyfriend, friends, Jill and team.

4. **Communication:** For Mike, the communication broke down with his mother at home and with his team. On the other hand, Jill handled the change well by communicating with her staff on a regular basis and offered support as required. Lisa also talked to people at work and home and did not hesitate to ask for help.

Of course, it's not always as simple as just applying the 4 Cs to a situation. Major and constant multiple changes can be overwhelming. It is vital therefore to draw on our resilience skills to maximise our personal resources and coping ability. Lisa did this by practicing yoga and relaxation.

Here is a quick summary of the 5 steps to positive change outcomes

STEP 1 – *Face the change, do not avoid or deny it.*

STEP 2 – *Approach it as an opportunity for growth.*

STEP 3 – *Nourish your physical body, think positive, let go of negative feelings.*

STEP 4 – *Separate what you can control, focus on this and let go of what you cannot.*

STEP 5 – *Communicate with others and seek information and support as needed.*

Now apply the 5 steps to the change that you are undergoing and look forward to enhancing your strength and repertoire of skills.

Story 8: United as a Team

Let's meet the team:

Firstly, **Ben**. He's sceptical, negative and hates his job. Then there's **Gary**. He's committed and gets on with the work. For **Claire**, a politics graduate with an eye to the future, this job is just a stopgap. She's looking for other work. As for **Jody**, she believes life is too short to take work seriously. She has her eye on Friday and the weekend. **Stuart** cannot wait to leave and start his new job. **Alice** cannot seem to knuckle down. She is slow, anxious, puts off decisions and always feels she is struggling to keep up with the rest of her colleagues. **Craig** is ambitious. He thinks he is a natural leader. **Delroy** wants to please and works hard to achieve results. Finally, **Pardip**. He could be seen as an ideal team member; after all, he's an innovator, a definite leader and no one could accuse him of lacking motivation or being unambitious. But there is such a thing as over-confidence, and nobody likes a know-it-all.

That is the team. Let us connect with them, as they start another day.

"What's wrong, Ben? I can see you're in a bad mood again."

Ben Jones took his eyes off the road momentarily and looked across to his wife, Alison, to reply. "Got a Team Away Day today doing team building, which means spending even more time with my colleagues than usual. Huh! I think it'll take a bit more than a stupid Away Day to improve how we work together! A complete waste of time, if you ask me."

"How come you're always moaning about the people you work with?" she responded.

"You should try doing my job one day. By lunchtime you'd feel like screaming too, believe me. I mean, it is not that hard to process loans. It's boring and monotonous. I hate it!"

Gary West arrived at work early; in fact, he always arrived *everywhere* early; it made him feel more relaxed. When he got in, he made himself a coffee, checked his emails and read the newspaper. By the time the rest of the staff arrived, he would be sitting at his desk, logged onto the system and ready to start. But this morning was different. There was a Team Building Day to attend. He was thrilled he was not going to be on the phone but doing something different. He wondered what that might be.

Gary was aware that some of the staff did not get on and that was affecting their performance, but it did not bother him. He just kept his head down, did his work and tried to ignore the politics. After all, if you worked for someone else, you had to put up with stuff you did not like. Gary just did not let it get him down.

In no more than 250 words, describe why you are ideally suited to this role. Claire Lucas despised job applications but working in a loan processing centre was not exactly a great career option for a twenty-four-year-old graduate. Looking at this application, she understood the job market was tough but had not realised quite how tough.

Fresh out of university, she had taken part-time employment at JS Loans, just to tide her over while she looked for a 'proper' job. Her friend Jody had been in the same boat, but here they both were, two years later, part-time work now full-time, with zero prospects of development. And here she was, on the train at eight o'clock in the morning, trying yet again to find the right words to impress a prospective employer. She had done interviews and filled in countless application forms, but so had thousands of other people in her position. It was getting her down; this combination of feeling useless and utterly bored with her job. At least today she would be away from the phone lines.

Briefly, she looked up from her application and wondered what the team-building activities would be like.

Jody Hayes closed her book and sighed. Four hundred pages, countless red herrings and finally the revelation that the victim had taken his own life rather than been murdered. What a cop out; all that build up, all those suspects, all those twists, all for nothing. She sat back and closed her eyes, hoping her disappointment would not leave her in a bad mood for the whole day. She had a date that evening and was keen to make a good impression on the man she had met at a nightclub the previous weekend. He had seemed nice. So nice she had thought of little else since. She had bored Claire senseless by talking about him continually. Jody thought Claire needed to lighten up. She was always moaning about work, but it was just a job. Life was more important than work, and what could be more important than a date with the man of her dreams?

This was it, the day he had been looking forward to, when he, Stuart Pitt, would finally tell his boss he was leaving. Twenty-one years old and finally his chance to move on to a real job. He'd worked for JS Loans for six months and had hated most of it: the rules; the people; the customers; the lot. But, there was a team-building meeting today, which meant there would be no calls to make and no targets to meet. Ahhh, great!

"They're going to pick on me," thought Alice. "As sure as eggs are eggs. And in any team-building exercise, I'm bound to be the guinea pig." She parked her car and slumped against the steering wheel, trying to delay the day ahead for a few more moments. She wanted to like her job and to build her career but she could not. At school, at home, in relationships, she just did not have faith in her own abilities. She believed she was slow at her work and did not want to get anything wrong, so took her time over everything. Her manager was always picking her up on her time-keeping. That was bad enough, but even worse were the snide comments that often came her way; comments about how she was holding the team back, not pulling her weight and how she was not very bright. Today was going to be a disaster.

Today was an opportunity for Craig Dawes. A perfect chance for him to demonstrate how he could confidently and maturely take control of a situation and lead a team of his own. He thought some of his colleagues did not get on and he wanted to impress them by helping them to work together. This would certainly earn him a feather in his cap. He looked in his bathroom mirror and was happy with what he saw. He had spent the previous evening reading about team structures and techniques for team building and he was looking forward to putting some of his ideas into action.

Being a second-hand car dealer had not suited Delroy Johnson at all. He wanted to keep this job at JS Loans, with its regular hours and decent pay packet; enough money to keep a roof over his and his three children's heads. At times he was irritated by the constant questions from customers but he kept that to himself. Delroy packed the plantain dish he'd prepared for the team. They enjoyed his food and he loved it when people showed their appreciation.

Pardip Singh was excited about the Team Building Day. He had only been in the job for a few months but was already full of ideas on how to improve things. JS Loans were just not making use of the latest business techniques. They seemed content to grind along in second gear which he found frustrating. What they needed, Pardip was convinced, was a daily get-together, assessment forms and he was sure innovation meetings would benefit the company. This Team Building Day was the perfect chance to get those ideas across. He hoped he could persuade his manager and colleagues to share his vision.

"Morning, everyone." Sandra Biggs greeted her team, who were sitting in a circle around her. Her senior managers had paid for a facilitator to come in and deliver the training. She had explained to the facilitator, Dom Swales, how the team was underperforming and instances of conflict in the group. She had told him about the arguments with staff who thought they knew better than her, about the lateness and about the members of staff who she sensed were not entirely happy with their jobs. She had also told him about the pressure she was getting from senior managers to turn things around and how it was difficult managing a workforce made up of people who would only be around for a few months.

"This is Dom." She introduced the man sitting on her left. "He's going to be taking today's session. Treat him nicely and I'm sure we'll all get a lot out of today."

"Thanks, Sandra," Dom said, in a soft West Country accent. "First let me tell you a bit about my background." He explained that before setting up his business, which was aimed at passing on his knowledge of team dynamics in the workplace, he had managed a large corporation.

"The purpose of today," he continued, "is to get you to work to a common goal and vision. I can see some of you are a little anxious, so let's start with a good old-fashioned icebreaker. You each have a pad and pencil. I would like you to write down your five favourite films and top five albums, please."

When the group read their choices out, they were surprised at the amount of common ground. Jody, Alice and Ben had chosen *The Bodyguard* and four members of the team had *Adele* on their lists. Dom grouped together the people with shared answers and asked everyone to list their favourite songs and actors. This time there was even more agreement.

Craig was especially surprised to discover that he shared not only his liking for Oasis with Gary, but they were both big fans of Robert Downey Jr. Dom put the people with shared interests together as he did before.

"Okay, we could talk about popular culture all day, but let's bring it into the work context. In your newly formed groups, list five things you like about working here and five things you don't."

Dom gave everyone fifteen minutes for the task. Plenty of noisy conversation followed. He asked everyone to share their likes and dislikes and wrote the list up on the board.

He moved on to the next phase of the day where he used a bright coloured tape to mark out a large square on the floor.

"This exercise is called Sculpting," he said. "The square represents your team. I want you to position yourself within it, in terms of where you feel you are in the team. Try not to think too much about it – just walk up to where it seems natural for you."

After some initial confusion, they made their way, one by one, to the square on the floor. Gary placed himself halfway between the centre and its edge. Claire went to a corner. She was followed by Jody. Pardip and Craig, with no hesitation, went to the centre. Delroy changed position a few times, eventually standing next to Gary.

"Your turn." Dom looked at Ben. "Where would you position yourself in the team?"

Ben did not walk into the square. "Here's just fine."

Stuart did the same; standing outside the square, but on the opposite side to Ben. Alice followed Ben's lead and remained outside the square.

Dom invited the team to share their feelings about their chosen positions, adding the new information to the earlier notes he had made on the board. He then split the team into groups and asked them to discuss the underlying reasons for their choices.

Dom always enjoyed this part of the day, as it gave him insight into the dynamics of the team. This was a team full of different personalities: leaders, diligent workers, as well as the few less enthusiastic members. But every team had those. His job was to harness the potential within the team.

He observed the team conversations. From the start, several people dominated the discussions. Pardip was contributing about ninety per cent of the conversation in his group. Stuart did the same in his. As Dom went around the groups, he encouraged the quieter members of the team to offer their opinions. When he asked Alice how she would improve the team, he expected the briefest of replies but she came up with several good ideas. Dom wondered if anyone had bothered to ask her opinion before.

"It's all about leadership. Every team needs a clear direction." Alice sounded nervous, but her words grabbed the group's attention. "I mean, surely we all want to enjoy our work, but that's not happening. People like Claire and Stuart want to leave because they're bored. Pardip wants to run the place and some of us just want to get on with our jobs. We're all different. What we need is a management strategy to get the best out of us and make us all feel part of the team. I'm sure we're all nice people; why should it matter if we all want different things, so long as we all work together to reach a goal?"

"That's a great observation, Alice. We're all different people, but we all want the same thing: to come to work, enjoy it, and do a good job," Dom said.

"Yes, but some people find it tedious," Claire said. "They'd like it to be more interesting and creative."

"True," agreed Alice, "But that doesn't mean you can't come in, do your best and try to enjoy it. It's just hard to do that when you don't feel valued. Imagine if, for example, somebody from Head Office came in every month and asked you about your job and what you want. That would make you feel better. It would no longer be a faceless company. You can't change the specifics of the job; we're processing loans, but you can change how we feel about it."

Dom smiled. It seemed that now Alice had opened up, there was no stopping her, and the rest of the team were expressing their thoughts and feelings about their work too. He glanced at his watch. One o'clock. As usual, whenever things got going, it was time to stop for lunch!

"Okay," Dom said. "We'll reconvene in an hour. Over lunch, think about a sentence that, in your opinion, encapsulates the vision of your company."

The group went through to the annex, where lunch was laid out for them. Delroy added his plantain dish to the table, inviting his colleagues to try his creation. Alice asked him how he had made it which led to other recipe exchanges and a discussion on spices and vegetables. Craig and Gary continued to talk affectionately about Oasis while munching on their sandwiches. Jody and Ben had an animated conversation about Kate Winslet in *Collateral Beauty*. They had twenty minutes left to come up with a sentence that reflected the vision of the company.

After lunch, Dom stood up in the middle of the room and clapped his hands. "Right, let's see what we've got. Which group wants to go first?"

Craig stood up, cleared his throat and announced, "JS Loans is the most innovative and customer-friendly lender in the country."

"Good stuff," Dom nodded. "I'm sure that's something your managers would agree with."

Next up was Stuart. "JS Loans wants to make as much money as possible, and if that means we all have to do menial jobs for a meagre wage, so what!" There was a burst of laughter from some of the team.

Then it was Delroy's turn. "JS Loans is fully committed to its staff and its employees."

And so, it went on. Some words cropped up repeatedly. Dom wrote them on the board at the front of the room: commitment, customers and profit, and variants on the themes like money, public, pro-active, etc.

Dom followed this with a question. "What are your core values in life?"

"What's the relevance of this to team building and work?" Claire asked.

"We spend a considerable amount of time at work. If what we do is not aligned to our intrinsic values, it will cause discontentment and affect our levels of engagement with our work," Dom replied.

"Mmm," said Claire. "I studied politics because I want to help people and make a difference in the world."

"All right, think about how what you do with JS loans helps people and makes a difference to them," said Dom.

"I like to make people happy," Delroy chipped in.

"Then, is what you do at work making a positive difference to people's lives and making them happy?" asked Dom.

"Of course, we're helping people to fulfil their needs through the loans and that should make them happy." And so, the discussion continued.

"Now, in your earlier groups, I want you to talk about your ideas of what is important to you in life, so you can fit in with the JS goals of profit, customers, and commitment. List what you can do to help the company enhance profits and remain committed to their employees and customers."

Dom loved to listen in on the discussions. He noticed a tangible change in the tone of the conversations. It was positive and nobody was dominating the discussions anymore. Everyone was having their say and offering constructive comments. Dom let the deliberations go on until he thought the team had exhausted their ideas.

"We are coming to the final part of the day. Let me ask you to please go back to the square on the floor which I mapped out earlier in the Sculpting exercise," Dom instructed.

The team shuffled up to the square without any hesitation.

Alice, though not in the middle, had at least moved herself into the square. Craig stayed in the centre, and Jody placed herself between Alice and Craig. Once more, Pardip headed straight for the middle and Stuart continued to stand outside of the square. Ben edged forward slightly inside the square while Gary and Delroy shifted a little closer than before to the centre.

The group shared their reasons for changing positions, describing how they felt more understood and closer to some of their team members.

"Now we have one last exercise. In your groups, I want you to come up with three things which in your opinion will help JS Loans achieve their aims," Dom said.

This led to another animated debate.

"I'm going to treat customers the same as how I'd like to be treated myself," said Claire.

"I'll try my best to help people," said Stuart, rather unconvincingly.

"I'm going to be committed to meeting the needs of my customers," said Gary.

"I will strive to do the best job that I can for my customers and my fellow members of staff," said Delroy.

"I will pass on my knowledge and help JS Loans become the market leader," said Pardip.

At the end of the session, Dom thanked everyone for coming and sought out Sandra for a feedback chat.

"You have got an interesting team there. Loads of good ideas, motivated members of staff with intelligent, constructive opinions. Yes, you've got a few, shall we say, less committed employees, but that is common. It's important to ensure today's ideas don't get forgotten and are followed up with consistent action."

Sandra smiled. She had been thinking exactly that. She had been involved in many training sessions that had been forgotten by the next morning. She would raise the new ideas in next week's managers' team-building meeting. She would make sure there were regular one-to-one meetings with staff, during which professional development would be assessed.

Ben was the first to leave. As he headed for the car park, he heard the loud chatter and laughter from the others. When he picked his wife up from work, he was smiling.

"Well, how was your day?" Alison asked.

"Actually, not as bad as I imagined it would be. I talked to Alice and Jody about my favourite films, something I've not done before. Nice women; you'd like them. I might share some more movie ideas with them to take some of the boredom out of work."

"Phew! I'm not used to you being happy at the end of your workday. I was anxious about getting in the car with you!" Alison admitted. "You were in a dreadful mood this morning."

The following day Gary came in as usual before everyone else. The next to arrive was Craig. Instead of walking past and muttering his usual half-hearted "Good morning", he went over to Gary and started chatting. Yesterday they had come up with quite a few ideas on increasing the targets and improving customer satisfaction levels.

Pardip arrived while they were talking and joined in the conversation on how they would present their ideas to Sandra. They also discussed involving Alice and Delroy, who had both come up with useful ideas the previous day.

At the next team meeting, Claire and Jody agreed to take on a little more responsibility. Ben did not protest or ridicule the ideas. Lately, everyone had noticed that he complained less than before and the way he chatted more to Alice and Jody, instead of keeping to himself.

Sandra had noticed these changes. She smiled to herself. Was this the beginning of a new, more united team?

*****

MORE ON TEAM BUILDING

Team building is about drawing out the best from team members despite their different skills, training, personalities and attitudes.

The icebreakers helped to open up conversations and find common ground for team members.

Sculpting was used in this case to draw out the relational dynamics of the team. Sculpting, commonly used in family therapy, can be very effective with workplace teams who can also benefit from a sense of belonging and common purpose. Sculpting can help to highlight and articulate issues and feelings that can be difficult to put into words, leading to new and positive behaviour.

There are other building blocks that help to create effective teams. These are:

- **Clear goals** – teams need to know what they should be doing
- **Openness** – members should feel able to discuss issues, with no damaging blame culture
- **Support and trust** – team members should help and support each other
- **Regular reviews** – feedback on how the team can improve their performance

For this organisation, the employee team-building was to be followed up by a management team-building day which would have addressed some of the following behaviours, which in turn would develop and maintain trust in the workplace:

- **No put-downs** – making points at the expense of others, making others look small and laughing at others destroys relationships and discourages involvement in the team

- **Give and take praise** – giving compliments and thanking others for their comments

- **Acknowledge others' views** – valuing comments made by other team members, not rejecting them out of hand, so as not to discourage members from sharing good ideas

- **Use humour** – a good sense of humour is a valuable asset for a team member/leader

- **Do not promote a blame culture** – teams that constantly allocate blame, end up destroying trust and limiting activity, as members are scared of making mistakes. Team members need to be able to take risks

- **Keep communicating** – when team members stop talking or avoid each other, the group will start to fragment

- **Avoid gossip** – gossip, rumours and talking about people destroys teams. Once the trust is lost, it is very difficult, and sometimes impossible to rebuild it

The style of management is crucial to the cohesiveness of a team. It is important to remember that team leaders must show no favouritism and should be consistent in mood, approach and behaviour, otherwise the team may lose focus and respect.

Finally, remember that *any* similar type of workforce is likely to suffer these types of problems. There are bound to be differing levels of commitment and no team-building exercise, however successful, will turn every single member of staff into a *perfect* employee!

Story 9: Rushes of Anger

Joe Barnes had a highly unusual problem. He was stood in the bathroom at the house of his local Member of Parliament, with a copious amount of blood running from the back of his left hand. Joe took a deep breath and tried to think what he could do.

Two hours earlier, he had been sat at his desk at the *Sotherton Gazette*, trying to write an article on the proposed bypass for the town. The proposal had been met with complaints by local residents who were concerned that it would create noise pollution and ruin local businesses. His feature for the following day's edition was about the pros and cons of building the new road. So far it largely comprised of quotes from local shop owners and interviews with members of the council. It was hardly looking like an award-winning article.

Joe welcomed the interruption when the phone rang giving him good news; his request to interview the Minister responsible for the bypass proposal had been swiftly met. A short drive later and Joe found himself sat in the drawing room of Vanessa Granger, Member of Parliament for Sotherton. Joe's day and prospects for his article were looking a lot brighter but it was then that his troubles began.

Vanessa Granger had been friendly enough and happy to answer some preliminary questions about her recent work and even made a few comments about her personal life. However, when the conversation moved on to the proposed bypass, she started to become uncooperative and abrupt.

"I'm not prepared to comment on that at this moment." This was her standard response to any question about the road. She would not give any opinions on the proposal or even comment on how it was developing. Joe was becoming increasingly frustrated and annoyed. He decided to try one last gamble.

"So, can you give us any indication of when a final decision will be made on the road? It's something our readers and indeed all local residents are desperate to know."

"It's too soon to say. I'm sorry; I can't answer that."

Joe stiffened in his seat, his heart was thumping and he could feel his face turning a bright shade of red. "Err, excuse me, I just need to pop to your bathroom for a moment."

Joe felt the rush of anger in his body, his steps faltering and making him feel faint as he made his way to the bathroom. Once inside, he slammed the door shut and punched the wall as hard as he could. He immediately regretted his action. He was hit by an intense pain and wanted to scream at the top of his voice. The more pertinent problem was the blood that was appearing on his hand. He had no idea how he was going to explain that to Mrs Granger.

In truth, it was not the first time that Joe's anger had spilled over in recent weeks. Three days earlier he had smashed a plate on his kitchen floor after a bad day at work. Just that morning he had almost crashed his car on the way to work after getting annoyed with a slow driver ahead of him. This was an altogether more serious situation though. He frantically tore off reams of toilet paper and wrapped it tightly around his hand in a desperate bid to stop the blood. It helped to an extent, but there was still a trickle coming out from his knuckles. He washed his hands in the sink and dried it with even more toilet paper.

"This will have to do," he thought. "She's going to wonder what I'm doing in here."

He made his way with trepidation back to Vanessa Granger and proceeded to ask inane questions about some issues in the town. Not surprisingly, she had started staring at his hand. Joe tried to explain the situation.

"Oh, it's a sports injury that's flared up. I played cricket at the weekend and got hit on the hand whilst batting."

"Weren't you wearing gloves?"

"Umm... no, it was during practice and I was just messing around, hitting a few balls. Silly really, should always wear gloves when a cricket ball is heading your way."

She did not look convinced but decided it was not worth pursuing the matter. The interview ended shortly after and Joe said his goodbyes, making his way out to his car.

"What am I going to tell the boss?" he worried.

Before leaving for the meeting, he had triumphantly told his editor that he was off to get an exclusive interview with Vanessa Granger and get her views on the bypass proposal. He sat in his car and looked over his notes. The main nuggets from the interview were that she was in favour of gay marriage, liked playing badminton twice a week and enjoyed listening to Pink Floyd. It was not exactly screaming 'Exclusive' at him. All of a sudden, his frustration boiled over and he thumped the steering wheel and screamed. A few seconds later, he was aware of Vanessa standing by the next car looking at him. "Great, she's going to think I'm insane," thought Joe. He pretended not to notice her and did his best to drive off calmly.

The most important time of the week for the *Gazette* was 1pm on a Friday. All of the writers gathered in the boardroom and Chief Editor Jerry Pickford finalised the content for that week's edition. It was a weekly publication so there were only six full-time employees and they each had to cover a variety of topics. In addition to being a features writer, Joe also had to write restaurant reviews and the television section of the paper. It was the features that he regarded as being the most important part of his job. He had always wanted to be a journalist and his ambition extended far beyond the confines of Sotherton.

He was approaching his fortieth birthday and was desperate for a national newspaper to give him an opportunity, but for him, time was running out. In truth, this had been the source of his recent anger outbursts. He had done his time with the *Gazette* and needed to move on. He did not want to spend his Friday lunchtimes listening to Jerry explaining that there would be a four-page feature on a farm show in that week's paper.

"We were going to lead with the lottery winner story," explained Jerry. "But our very own Joseph Barnes has just returned from a meeting with Vanessa Granger so we may have a last-minute change to the front page." Everybody looked at Joe.

"Err, yeah, it was an interesting interview."

"Did you get all the low-down on the bypass?"

Joe explained that he did not get the low-down on the bypass. In fact, he did not get much of a low-down on anything.

"She likes badminton and Pink Floyd?" Jerry asked. "How on earth is that going to be front page news?"

"We could use 'loser' in the headline. That seems apt."

It was Ray Broad, another writer for the paper and a constant source of irritation for Joe. Ray never missed a chance for a sarcastic comment and relished winding Joe up. He had been the one to pen the story of the local resident who had recently won £3,000,000 on the National Lottery. The story that was currently going to be front page of the next edition.

"Thanks for that, Ray. Any cleverer remarks?"

"Comfortably dumb?" Ray suggested this with a smirk on his lips, getting a bigger laugh from the rest of the room.

"Oh, just shut up, Ray," snapped Joe. "I've had illnesses more amusing than you. You're thirty, you live with your parents and look like a hippy student with anorexia. If anybody should be getting laughed at here, it's you." The anger was bubbling up inside him, but before it could go any further Jerry slapped his hand on the boardroom table.

"Joe, I think you better go outside for a bit and calm yourself down. Ray, less of the wisecracks. We're here for serious work and not to listen to your stand-up comedy routines."

Joe stormed out of the room, straight to the smoking area behind the building. He did not smoke, but often came out here to try and calm himself down. "Christ, I need a new job," he thought. "I'm fine away from here; this place is driving me mad."

Jerry poked his head out of the door. "Joe, we need to have a chat. What happened in there isn't acceptable. I know Ray can be a pain, but there's no reason to react like that. We're far too busy to deal with it this afternoon, so make sure you finish off the piece on Granger, then go home. I want to see you first thing on Monday." With that, Jerry went back inside, leaving Joe to contemplate his future.

"C'mon, Joe. Let's get an early wicket, mate." It was Saturday afternoon and Joe was doing what he enjoyed the most: playing cricket for Sotherton. In his former years he had been a talented fast bowler and had almost made it as a professional. Twenty years later, his hair was receding and he ached for days after playing but he could still bowl effectively for his local team and was preparing to open the bowling in the first league fixture of the season. His first ball was exactly what he hoped it would be. The batsman made a nervous attempt to play the ball, missed it and the ball thudded into the wicketkeeper's gloves.

"Great start, Joey. Keep it there," shouted one of the fielders.

Joe looked at the batsman, a young man, fresh out of university and aiming to make a name for himself, who smirked and stared at Joe in return. Joe read this as a sign that this guy was not afraid of him and felt he could score runs off him easily enough. "We'll see about that," he thought.

Joe decided he would try some intimidation with the next ball. He delivered a bouncer aimed at his head. He steamed ahead to bowl and hurled the ball down the pitch as fast as he could. The batsman calmly ducked under the ball and stared back at Joe, the same slight smirk on his lips. Suddenly Joe was imagining the batsman was Ray Broad, rival journalist and all-round annoyance, not just some young upstart cheeky batsman. "Revenge," thought Joe. Revenge for the way Ray had spoken to him the previous day.

For the rest of the over, Joe tried his hardest to bowl as fast as he could and hit the batsman somewhere on his body. Unfortunately, the batsman was more than up to the challenge and comfortably dealt with the attack, even despatching one ball to the boundary for four.

At the end of the over, Joe's captain trotted over to him. "Great pace, but try and pitch it up, he likes the bouncers. Try and do what you did with the first ball."

Joe was barely listening, as this had become personal. 'Ray' needed to be taken down a peg or two and a cricket ball was just the thing to do it with. Two unsuccessful overs later, his captain had had enough. "What are you doing, Joe? He's taking you to the cleaners; you're just bowling a load of rubbish. Sorry, mate, I'm taking you off. We can't keep conceding these runs."

Joe was seething. You could hear the sound of his teeth grinding. He hated failure and he hated being told he was not good enough.

"Give me one more over. I can get him out."

"Sorry, Joe, you need a break." Somewhere deep within him, Joe felt he may be right, but found it difficult to admit that.

"Need a break? You don't know what you're doing! I'm your best player by a mile."

"Joe! You're not bowling anymore. I'm in charge here and that's my decision."

"Well, if that's your decision, this is my decision! See you later." He turned round and stomped off the field.

"What the hell do you think you're doing?" his captain shouted after him.

Joe did not turn round, but simply waved his hand in the air. "I've had enough of this. You can't captain to save your life, so I'm dammed if I'm going to stand around fielding all afternoon. I've got far better ways to spend my weekends."

He staggered to the changing room and slammed the door shut behind him. He picked up items of equipment he could see and hurled it at the wall in a rage, before slumping on a bench, holding his head in his hands in exasperation.

"What's happening to me? It's a game of cricket, I love playing this game." He surveyed the damage in the changing room. Joe began to realise that his problem was not just confined to his working life. Jerry Pickford liked to make his employees feel at ease when he had an important issue to discuss with a staff member. He often opted to invite them for a walk around the town with the individual in question. So, the following Monday morning, Joe found himself strolling around Sotherton with Jerry.

"I think you know what this is about, Joe."

"I can have a good guess."

"Yes, well, it's becoming a serious issue. I can't have a member of staff losing their cool in the workplace, and Friday wasn't an isolated incident."

"I know, Boss, I'm very sorry. I'm just having a tough time at present."

"At home? Everything okay with the wife?"

"Err, yeah, fine, I suppose."

"So it's work?"

Joe sighed. "I guess."

"Look, you are a quality writer and an asset to the *Gazette*, but you can't keep snapping at people and throwing your toys out of the pram. Plus, we've had a complaint from Vanessa Granger. Apparently, there were blood stains on the wall of her bathroom after your visit."

Joe's face turned a bright red. He tried to think of a plausible lie but nothing occurred to him. After a few seconds of silence, Jerry decided to put him out of his misery.

"Look, I'm not interested in what happened. I just don't want it happening again."

"It won't."

"But it might." Jerry took something out his pocket. "I want you to give this woman a call."

He passed a laminated business card to Joe.

Rachel Stone
Stress and Anger Management Coaching
Call now for support

"I'm happy to let you see her during work time. As far as I'm concerned, if we can get you performing as I know you can, then I don't mind you having a few hours off."

Joe felt strangely relaxed about this news. In his heart, Joe knew he had a problem and wanted to get it sorted out. It was embarrassing to discuss but Jerry had taken the lead and offered his full support. Joe felt compelled to do what he could to justify Jerry's faith in him.

"Thanks, Boss. I won't let you down."

"What's your earliest recollection of your anger getting out of control?" Rachel Stone didn't look like an anger management coach. In fact, Joe thought she looked like a farmer. She was wearing tight blue jeans, a tartan patterned shirt and had her hair in a tight bun.

Joe pondered on the question. It was halfway through his third session and after a few moments of small talk, Rachel Stone had launched in with a big question.

"Not sure. I mean, I had tantrums when I was a little kid and a few teenage strops, but who doesn't? Brother kicks your football into the road, mum won't let you have chips, all the usual stuff. In our house my mum always listened to my brother and he was always right as he was older than me. After a while I gave up and stopped speaking up for myself even though a lot of things made me angry."

Joe turned his gaze away from Rachel and went quiet for a few moments. "That was lonely," he continued sadly. Rachel smiled reassuringly.

The rest of the session was spent discussing various other aspects of Joe's life; his childhood, his relationships, his family, even his social life. She seemed very keen to find out more about his formative years and his quest to become a professional sportsman.

"I don't want to sound arrogant, but I was the best. School, Club and District; I was better than everyone else. Right up until I was eighteen."

"What happened next?"

Joe took a deep breath. "I had a trial for my county, a chance to become a professional. I was going to make loads of money and play for England." He took a long pause. "Then they rejected me. Said I wasn't quite good enough and that they didn't need to see me again."

"How did that make you feel?"

"Angry." Joe's answer was instant.

"Tell me a bit more about this anger."

Joe considered. "Partly I was angry at them for rejecting me, but mainly I was angry at myself. I'd focused so much on becoming a pro, I'd just assumed it was going to happen. My whole life was mapped out...so when it all fell apart I didn't know what to do. I'd been average at school and I wasn't really interested in learning. Who cares about Shakespeare when you're going to be playing in the Ashes in a few years' time?"

"Sounds like this really knocked your confidence."

"I didn't know what I wanted anymore. I had a few agency jobs, dabbled in drugs and I probably wasn't much fun to be around. I felt as if I had lost my way completely. The worst thing is I didn't tell anyone at home as my brother would only have made fun of me and my mum would have taken his side anyway. I didn't have any close mates either but even if I did, you don't really talk about those sorts of things."

Clearly, they were on to something, so Rachel spent the rest of the session discussing this period of Joe's life.

By the end of the session, Joe thought that Rachel could be his biographer. Rachel explained that in the next sessions they would work at resolving the source of the anger issues and look at coping strategies. She smiled reassuringly at Joe.

To Joe's astonishment, he found himself looking forward to the following week's session. He was not entirely sure why, but he arrived for the session fifteen minutes early. He was interested in what Rachel was going to talk about.

"We all face challenges and difficulties. Getting positive outcomes from that is all about our approach to the challenges. You vent your anger but in a negative way. You take out your frustrations on things around you and that leads to negative outcomes."

Joe nodded slowly. This was making sense, even if the words weren't exactly comforting.

"What we need to do is to get you expressing your anger and emotions in positive, safe ways."

"How do we do that?" Joe asked slowly. Rachel smiled.

Over the next week, Joe came round to the idea that deep down his issues were stemming from that cold April afternoon twenty-two years ago. Had he ever got over that rejection? Had he ever found another passion? Was he still bitter? The more Joe considered the questions, the more he realised that his unfulfilled ambition with professional sport was the real cause of his anger issues. Which was progress at least, but he still had no idea how he was going to solve the problem. However, he had faith in Rachel. She was friendly, helpful, and more importantly, sounded like she knew what she was talking about.

"Lie back on the couch and close your eyes." Joe did as he was told. Once he felt that he was in a relaxed position, Rachel continued.

"Now, picture an image that you find soothing."

For reasons he could not fathom, the image of a colourful butterfly suddenly appeared in his head.

"Focus your attention on it steadily. Study the details of the object, the colours, shapes, shades etc."

This lasted for around ten minutes. Rachel slowly repeated her instructions until Joe felt completely at ease. When the exercise finished, Rachel went back to discussing Joe's life, his past and his current issues. She went through some more relaxation techniques and explained how they could help Joe stop his anger from manifesting and hurting other people.

This pattern continued for a few more weeks. Rachel would spend the first part of the session passing on a relaxation or meditation exercise to Joe, then they would discuss Joe's situation and look for solutions. Over time, Joe learnt that it was okay to give himself permission to express anger, but it needed to happen through safe, healthy methods.

The running he had taken up in the last few weeks was helping and so did the relaxation techniques he was learning. Some of them he found too left-field, but others were extremely useful. He was determined to use them when difficult situations arose.

"Hey, Joe, got any bigger exclusives for us? Maybe a local council member is into squash?" Ray shouted the words across the office floor as Joe entered the room.

"Nice one, Ray," he calmly replied and walked over to his desk. For the next few minutes, all he could hear was Ray making snide remarks in his direction. Joe closed his eyes and pictured the butterfly, its beautiful colours, its graceful motions and its perfect shape. He opened his eyes. Strangely, he could not hear Ray anymore, everything was peaceful. He typed away diligently for the next fifteen minutes, until his desk phone started ringing.

It was Jerry. "Joe, can you come to my office for a few minutes please?" He put the phone down before Joe had a chance to reply. He calmly locked his computer and trotted off to Jerry's office.

Jerry had his business face on and did not offer a smile as Joe entered the room. "Take a seat," he said solemnly. There was a thin, brown folder on his desk and he looked at it intently.

"Now, you know we've discussed your anger issues and over the last month you've been seeing an anger management coach to help with that. Firstly, I need to thank you for your co-operation. I hope the coaching is going well. Secondly, I had to report your issues to the publishing group as it was a disciplinary issue. Human Resources have come back to me and unfortunately we need to go through disciplinary proceedings."

"What does that mean?"

"It means two things. First of all, it's an official warning. Anymore anger outbursts and your role here could become untenable. Secondly, it means that we need to have regular meetings to discuss your conduct. That is until we have a track record of you working well and without incident for several months. Clear?"

Joe looked Jerry in the eye. "Perfectly clear, Boss. Whatever it takes, I won't let you down."

Jerry looked back at Joe. "Good, now get back to work."

Joe left the office and went back to his desk. He closed his eyes for a few seconds and thought of the butterfly again. There were no rushes of anger anymore. He felt calm and back in control of his life.

*****

MORE ON ANGER MANAGEMENT

Joe's anger problem started in his youth when he was rejected for the cricket team at eighteen. It is at this point that he needed to learn to express his anger in healthy ways. However, this did not happen and there could be several reasons for this. Perhaps because there is a stigma attached to showing disappointment, as this may be seen as weak and a failure. Displaying anger is often seen as being a negative behaviour. It would have helped Joe if at eighteen, he had trusting relationships where he could open up and share his feelings. This could have been a school counsellor, a teacher, a parent, a sibling or a friend.

It is important to share with someone you can trust fully and who will keep your information confidential. Talking helps to release the anger from your body. Also, you cannot make sense of some things if you cannot see them. Talking helps to 'let it out' so we can 'see it' and make sense of it and gain other perspectives. Solutions may not emerge from this but the process of letting it out and being heard is therapeutic in itself. Uncontrollable anger and depression are often the results of a build-up of 'unspoken' emotions over a period of time.

Do you have at least three people to whom you can open up and bare your soul and who will keep this confidential? Someone who will just listen and not judge you. Think about this for a few moments. If you have less than three, then try this:

Make a list of everyone you know: family, friends, colleagues, neighbours, acquaintances, etc.

Now pick out a few who are supportive and have listened without criticising you. What is the worst thing that will happen if you share your problems with these people? If there are no repercussions and this feels okay, then spend more time with these people and develop two-way open and trusting relationships. It is good to have at least three people like this as one or two may not be available for various reasons. If you cannot come up with three, then consider using a professional like a counsellor/coach. The important thing is that feelings are expressed soon after difficult experiences, otherwise they build up over time and may get out of control like it did for Joe.

Also reflect on your beliefs about anger. What were the messages you were picking up about anger as you were growing up from the significant people in your life? Were you given the permission to be angry without any consequences? Do you think it is bad or weak to be angry? We are human so we will all feel angry at some point in our lives. We should give ourselves the permission to express it but in healthy ways such as talking to people we trust, writing it out (like Neil does in 'The New Man' in Story 11 and Paul in 'Built for Resilience' in Story 3) or diffusing it with relaxation and breathing techniques.

Here is one breathing technique particularly good for anger:

Breathe out through your mouth in short bursts 10 times. Then breathe normally. Repeat until anger has subsided. Stop if you feel dizzy. Let your breathing settle before you repeat it.

Jerry had the qualities of a firm and fair manager. He 'nipped the issue in the bud' and sought help for Joe before it escalated. He also dealt with it formally.

If Jerry had not offered the support at that point to Joe, what might have been the consequences for Joe and within the team? Take a few moments to reflect on that.

Story 10: In the Here and Now

"Malcolm ... it's time."

Malcolm stirred. He buried his head deeper into the duvet and chose to ignore the call.

"Mal ... colm! Mal, get up!!"

Malcolm tried to make sense of the fuzzy jumble in his head and sat up suddenly, with a jolt.

"Oh, it's Monday, oh no!" He slid back under the covers.

"Mal!! Malcolm, get up, for God's sake. You're going to be late for work," his wife shouted from downstairs. "I'm getting breakfast for Molly and she'll be late for school again if you don't get up now."

For the past few months, this had been the regular weekday morning routine for Malcolm's family, and with each day it was getting worse.

As Malcolm drove into the car park at work, his heart was pounding so hard, he thought it would jump out of his chest. His stomach felt like a tightly twisted bundle of rope. As he parked up, he felt the warm beads of sweat on his hands. His mind slipped into overdrive as he sat in his car trying to overcome the dread of walking into work.

"Oh God, give me the strength. I have to go through that door. If I don't, I'll lose my job, then how would I pay the mortgage? What if we lose our house? Alice will leave me, and Molly, what about Molly? I can't bear to think about all this."

He summoned up the strength to haul his body, which felt like a ton of bricks, across the car park and into the entrance of his workplace. He hurried to his desk, head down, shoulders slouched over his chest.

From the corner of his eye, he saw Barry, his manager, coming towards him.

"Good morning, Malcolm, you're late again. Can we have a few minutes in my office, please?"

Barry closed his office door and saw Malcolm's stooped, nervous figure, fumbling with the chair, trying awkwardly to sit down. Before Barry had time to get behind his desk, he heard a great, shuddering sob. He turned and saw Malcolm shaking and weeping, his face buried in his hands.

Barry felt embarrassed. "Erm, I think you need to go home and calm down, take a few days off, try to get yourself into a fit state to work. I think you should make an appointment with your doctor. Would you like me to ask one of your colleagues to go with you to your car, make sure you're, erm, all right?"

Malcolm staggered out into the car park, alone. The thought of allowing any of his workmates to see him in such a state made him shudder with shame. They would think he was pathetic, a wimp. No, there was no way he would ever let anyone see him like this.

Instead of going home, he drove into the car park of the Leisure Centre on his way. He parked up in a quiet spot in the corner.

"Please, God, help me, what's the matter with me? What can I do?" He started sobbing again. He wanted to scream but resisted the temptation.

"What shall I say to Alice?" An hour passed. He could not sit there forever. He took a deep, trembling breath and slowly made his way home.

"I'm not feeling well," he muttered as he walked in through the front door. Avoiding Alice's eye, he went into his study and stayed there until Molly came home from school.

On Barry's advice, Malcolm made an appointment with his doctor. He spent most of his time in his study, staring at nothing. He had no appetite, his sleep was patchy and disturbed, and he kept out of Alice's way.

After getting Malcolm to complete a questionnaire, the doctor said Malcolm was suffering from stress and anxiety, signed him off work and suggested he see Jonathan, the Mindfulness Practitioner who was part of the Wellbeing Service at the surgery.

Once he started to answer Jonathan's questions, all Malcolm's fears and anxieties poured out of him in an uncontrollable torrent.

"It's Molly, my eight-year-old daughter; she had meningitis two years ago and we nearly lost her. Alice, my wife, hasn't been the same since. She's changed. She's not interested in me or our friends. But I don't blame her, I am always in a bad mood when I come in from work. I don't want to fly off the handle but something comes over me and I just can't help it. The other day I even shouted at Molly and felt guilty afterwards, I cried in bed. At this rate, Alice will soon get fed up with me and leave."

There was a long pause after which Malcolm continued. "Maybe I deserve it. I'm no good for her while I'm in this state. I feel so ashamed. I'm letting my family down. I'm a man, for heaven's sake, I should be able to cope."

"I can see it has been tough for you at home, Malcolm," Jonathan responded. "How are things at work?"

"Work has been a nightmare for the past few years too; changes and more changes, one after the other. I've had three different managers in the past two years. I'm expected to know what to do without any training and to justify every move I make. I told my last manager that I need more training and more time to reach my targets, but he said everyone is in the same position. My current manager has put me on a performance plan and offered coaching but the coach has cancelled twice. Anyway, the coaching is going to be useless; it's not going to help me with the specialist nature of my work. It's just ticking the boxes for them. There is no way I can do the number of jobs they're asking me to do in a day unless I can be in two places at the same time or fly from one job to the next.

"I don't know what to do; I feel trapped and frightened. I feel weak and pathetic. I should be able to cope and look after my family. Now I'm off sick with stress, so work have a good excuse to get rid of me, don't they? How will we pay the mortgage? Alice will think I am useless and leave me. I won't have anything left. I don't know what to do. I've locked myself in my office at home for the past few days not wanting to face her or face up to my problems because I don't know how to. And I don't want to lose my temper with either of them. Alice only speaks to me if she has to; the rest of the time we just keep out of each other's way. The doctor suggested medication or talking to you. I don't want medication if I can help it." Malcolm's eyes filled with tears. He reached for the box of tissues on the side table next to his chair.

"Has Alice ever said that she's going to leave you?" Jonathan asked.

Malcolm looked up, blew his nose and replied, "Not in so many words, no, but …"

"Okay, Malcolm, I'm going to help you to get out of this negative thinking downward spiral. At the moment, there's nothing to say that Alice is going to leave you or you are going to lose your job, so we will stay with the fact that at this moment in time you have both. Do we agree on that?"

Malcolm gave a hesitant nod.

"Now tell me, Malcolm, which scenario depicts the strong man of the house; the one where you lock yourself in your study at home and refuse to face the world, or the one where you speak to someone who can help you to make sense of your inner turmoil and try some ways of resolving your problems?"

Jonathan gave Malcolm a few moments to think until he admitted that the second scenario depicted more strength.

"It is easier said than done though, Jonathan. I had to summon up all the courage I had to walk in here this morning."

"Yes, but you had the guts to do it and you've proved you can be strong. Do you have any other questions? Is there anything else you're anxious about?"

"No, I don't think so." Malcolm shook his head.

"Shall we make a start on the first mindfulness practise then?"

"Anything that will get me out of this rut."

"Just listen to my voice and follow the instructions as best as you can and settle in at your own pace. The important thing is that you don't overthink what you're doing, as that defeats the object of the practice. Are we ready to make a start?"

Malcolm nodded. Jonathan took him through the practice, slowly, pausing whenever necessary.

"Now sit back. You can close or lower your eyes. Focus your attention on your breath and just be aware of the movement that your breath is making in your body. Now notice the contact of your body with the surface of the chair you are sitting on. Can you feel the air on your bare arms? Notice the taste in your mouth, and now focus again on the movement of the breath in your chest. If you can, try and take your breath a bit deeper and just focus on the movement again. When you are ready, you can open your eyes."

When Malcolm opened his eyes, Jonathan asked him how he felt.

"I feel a little calmer," Malcolm responded, his voice a fraction less shaky than before.

"After a short break, would you like to try another exercise?"

"Okay," Malcolm said. "I'd like to pop to the bathroom first." On his return, Malcolm had a drink from the glass of water by his side and indicated that he was ready to start again.

Jonathan said, "We'll do an object meditation. This one is about taking and absorbing your attention on a pleasing object or sound around you. This takes the attention away from your negative thoughts to the object or sound and stops you spiralling into unhealthy thoughts and feelings. Look around this room. Does any object catch your eye?"

Malcolm looked around the room and stopped at a picture on the wall depicting a calming image of golden sunlight shining through green, lush trees.

Jonathan instructed gently:

"Focus your attention on this picture; notice the colours, shapes and every detail of the image. Keep your attention on this image for five minutes. You can practise this for longer at home, if you have the time. You can do the same with music, immersing yourself fully for several minutes at a time."

Malcolm followed Jonathan's instructions. After the five minutes had elapsed, he said, "I can do this with the trees I can see from my office window. And I love music, but I haven't listened to it for ages; I think I need to get back to my music."

Jonathan returned Malcolm's smile. "Whenever you start worrying about Alice or Molly or your job," he said, "just focus on your breath, senses, sounds and attractive or interesting objects. This will help you to feel calmer and stop the worrying spiral of negative thoughts. I'd like you to work on this until we meet again in a few weeks."

After two weeks, Malcolm walked in and sat down for the second session. Jonathan noticed that his posture was much better. "How are you today, Malcolm?" he asked.

Malcolm took a few moments to reflect before he replied. "I must say, I was sceptical about all this mindfulness stuff before I came to see you, but I think it's helping and I can feel a difference. I've managed to practise the breathing and object meditation. I meant to listen to some music but haven't had the time for that yet. Anyway, I've slept a little better this week. Obviously, it's not quite the miracle I hoped for, instantly taking away all my worries, but I definitely feel a little calmer."

Jonathan chuckled. "No miracles in my bag, Malcolm, but if you want to stay on this path, I can offer more mindfulness techniques that will build on your progress."

"Okay, so what's next?" Malcolm asked.

"This one is called the Body-Scan Meditation. Are you ready to begin? You might like to use the blanket I've left by your chair as it can get quite cold remaining still for an extended period. We'll do this in a seated position here, but at home it can be performed lying down."

At Malcolm's cue, Jonathan started to go through the exercise, again pausing at appropriate moments and allowing Malcolm to settle into the practice gradually.

Body-Scan Meditation *(Adapted from script by Jon Kabat-Zinn)*

"Let your arms be comfortable by your sides or in your lap. Start by just noticing the weight of your body and how it feels against the chair or mat.

"Continuing to notice the feeling of sitting or lying, each time you exhale, imagine yourself sinking a little deeper into a comfortable state.

"As with other meditation techniques, it's quite normal for your attention to wander away from your breath and body occasionally. Don't be concerned when this happens – just gently lead your awareness back to your body scan.

"Begin noticing your breathing – where it enters your nostrils or mouth maybe or perhaps deep in your lungs, above your diaphragm. If you place your hand just above your stomach and feel the gentle rise and fall of your breath, that is your diaphragm. This is a very good place to notice your breath. Perhaps by

placing a hand over your abdomen, you may notice what seems like a gentle rise or expansion as you breathe in and a lowering or contraction as you breathe out. Continue just noticing your breathing for a little while.

"After a while, start to move your focus away from your breathing and down your left leg, down to your knee and then down to your ankle and your left foot and then to the big toe of your left foot. Notice how it feels; is it cold or warm? Do you notice the sensation of contact with your sock or do you feel air around it? Now expand your awareness to your little toe and then all the toes in between. What sensation do you notice in them? If you don't notice any feelings, that's quite okay. Just be aware of whatever you notice or don't notice!

"Once again, be aware of your breathing. Imagine your breath travelling right down your body and down your left leg and into your toes. When you breathe out, imagine your breath travelling back up your leg and up your body until it leaves your nose. From now on, do the same sort of breathing into each part of your body that you focus on.

"Now let your awareness extend into the whole of your left foot including the ball, the sole and the heel. Then the ankle, the sides, the upper part and the whole of your left foot. Breathe right down into the whole of your left foot and then right out again.

"*Extend that gentle and welcoming awareness into the lower part of your left leg. Up to your left knee and then the upper part of your left leg. Perhaps your left leg may feel a little different to your right leg now. If so, just be aware of that.*

"*Now start to move your awareness down your right leg, down to your knee and then down to your ankle and your right foot and then to the big toe of your right foot. Notice how it feels; is it cold or warm? Do you notice the sensation of contact with your sock or do you feel air around it? Now expand your awareness to your little toe and then all the toes in between. What sensation do you notice in them?*

"*Once again, be aware of your breathing. Imagine your breath travelling right down your body and down your right leg and into your toes. When you breathe out, imagine your breath travelling back up your leg and up your body until it leaves your nose.*

"*Now let your awareness extend into the whole of your right foot including the ball, the sole and the heel. Then the ankle, the sides, the upper part and the whole of your right foot. Breathe right down into the whole of your right foot and then right out again.*

"*Extend that gentle, curious and welcoming acceptance into the lower part of your right leg. Up to your right knee and then the upper part of your right leg.*

"Now slowly bring your awareness up to your pelvis, your hips, groin, and buttocks. Once again, breathe down into that area and imagine that you are bathing that part of your body with refreshing and nourishing oxygen.

"Continue to extend your awareness up the trunk of your body into your lower back and abdomen. Be aware of your diaphragm rising as you breathe in and contracting as you breathe out. Once again, breathe down into that area and notice any emotions or physical sensations and explore their meaning, if any, for you. Focus on breathing down into any discomfort or pain you may feel in any part of your body. Rather than breathing the pain away, work towards acceptance and gentle awareness of any discomfort in your body.

"Now move your awareness up into your chest and your upper back. Notice your breathing in your chest and, if you can, notice your own heart beating. Welcome any emotions and physical feelings and listen for any messages that you think these sensations may have for you.

"Then move to the hands and the arms, noticing both at the same time, from the tips of the fingers right up to the shoulders. Once again, breathing right down to the fingertips of each arm and back up the body again.

"Next, focus awareness back up into the shoulders and up into the neck, the jaw, noticing any tension there. Then into the rest of *the face and up into the forehead, temples and scalp. Often here is where tension is stored.*

"While remaining fully mindful of all experiences in a slow and gentle manner, finally arrive at the very top of the head. You might choose to imagine that you can breathe in from the very top of your head and let your breath flow right down your body, to the tips of your toes and then right back up and out of the very top of your head. Allow that to happen a few times with an awareness of your body being refreshed and renewed – as if your batteries are being recharged.

"Continue for a few minutes to bathe in this sense of energising refreshment and then just remain aware of your body and breathing. Reflect on the process that you have undertaken here and any sense of peace in mind and body that it leaves you with.

"Thank yourself for allowing the time to experience this journey and contemplate your return to whatever you will be doing shortly.

"Reflect on your experience and get ready to open your eyes and have a stretch before sharing your thoughts.''

Malcolm blinked a few times before slowly opening his eyes. "I got some of that but not all of it and lost you somewhere in the middle," he said quietly. "I am feeling good though. I can't remember feeling this relaxed for a long time."

Jonathan rose from his chair and reached out to a shelf by his desk. He picked up a CD and a handout and passed them over to Malcolm.

"This one takes more practice and you can do that with this CD at home. You could also get Alice to read the script or make your own recording. There are other audio relaxation recordings on our website which the receptionist can give you. The state of relaxation will begin to feel more familiar as you practice this regularly. Hopefully you will notice an improvement in your concentration levels, feel more centred and in control of your situation at home and at work. I look forward to seeing you again in four weeks this time. That should allow you more time to practice what we have been working on and consider ways of managing your issues at work and home."

One evening, a few weeks later, Malcolm spoke to his wife. "Alice ... how long are we going to keep ignoring each other, not facing up to our problems? We need to talk, be a family again like we were before." He felt a lump in his throat, swallowed and continued. "I miss that terribly. What do you say?"

Alice walked away into the kitchen without a word. However, a few minutes later she came back, brushed her hand softly against his, giving him an awkward smile.

When Alice came downstairs after her shower the next morning, Malcolm was busy in the kitchen.

"I'm bored with cereal and milk every morning. Time to have something tasty and warm!" he said as he beat the eggs for an omelette.

Alice's eyes wondered over to the dining table where the table was set for three people to enjoy a hot, delicious breakfast. "Molly ... come down for breakfast," Malcolm heard her call out.

Later that week Malcolm noticed that he was not as anxious about returning to work. He thought about walking through the front gate and although his chest tightened a little, he felt it was now possible. The next day Malcolm sent an email to his manager, confirming a meeting with him for the following week.

At the meeting, Malcolm let out a long sigh as he was told that he was not going to lose his job. His manager said he could start back on a phased return. Relieved, he bought a bunch of flowers for Alice on his way home and a new dress for Molly. That week he vacuumed the lounge and tidied his office. Even though he had been off work up until then, he had not felt inclined to do anything around the house. He sensed that his real self was beginning to resurface after ages.

Malcolm sat down for the third session with Jonathan.

"Alice, Molly and I went out shopping for the first time in two years. Alice is still not saying much but I reckon I'm more tolerable these days. I haven't had an outburst at home since I last saw you and have had more energy to help around the house. I actually cooked the Sunday dinner last week; something I haven't felt like doing since Molly's illness."

"That's good news, Malcolm." Jonathan smiled. "In this session I would like to reinforce the techniques we have already worked on and talk about some mindfulness practices that you can integrate into your normal everyday routine. Does that sound okay?"

"That sounds good. I need to check out if I have been doing the long body scan in the right way but I'm fine with the small techniques we worked on in the first session."

"Alright, we'll practice the body scan first." Jonathan agreed and went over the whole exercise again, ensuring that Malcolm was following the instructions correctly. They discussed tangents of the practice until Malcolm felt he fully understood the technique.

For the next technique, Jonathan handed Malcolm a bowl of dried fruit, chocolate and nuts and asked him to pick what he wanted and eat it. They continued the discussion while Malcolm finished eating a honey-coated almond.

Jonathan said, "This time I would like you to eat a second almond in silence and really notice the texture and flavours in your mouth. Eat it as slowly as possible."

When Malcolm had finished eating, Jonathan asked if he had noticed any difference between eating the first and second almond.

"Well, it's obvious really. I noticed the flavours more and the difference between the taste of the honey and almond the second time round. I think you're suggesting that if I do this at mealtimes, I should feel more satisfied with my meals?"

"That's right. You'll feel more satisfied and, hopefully you'll eat less, because you're eating slowly. In addition, the digestion of your meal would be enhanced because the nutrients are better absorbed in your body. I understand that you're busy and it may not be possible with every meal but try and do it with at least one meal a day."

"I need to get away from my desk at lunch anyway, so I will from now on take my lunch to my car and eat my sandwich mindfully. Breakfast and dinner are impossible as the attention is all on getting Molly to eat."

"That's a good plan, Malcolm. I would like you to think about doing everything more mindfully; for example, walking. Be aware of each step that you take and the rise and fall of each step. You can adapt this when walking from one meeting to the next or walking from the car park to the supermarket."

"I have a long walk to the toilets at work."

"There you go then, a mindful walk to the toilets! You can do every task in your day with more presence, awareness and focus, even things like the washing up, having a shower, cleaning and so on. Do you think you can work on that?"

"Of course. It doesn't take any extra time and it's simple."

On that note, they agreed to meet for the final session in another four weeks' time.

Jonathan used the final session to recap on everything that had been covered previously. He invited Malcolm to ask questions until he was confident he would be able to practise the techniques on his own.

"We have ten minutes left of our time. Is there anything you want to talk about before we end the sessions?"

"Well, you were right to say that my focus and concentration is likely to improve so my targets at work are fractionally better. I had my first meeting with the coach at work and it wasn't as fruitless as I had anticipated. I'll give it a chance and see where we go from there. I'll certainly do my best to keep all this up. I can feel the difference and see the sense in it.

"Also, I would like to say how much I appreciate that you didn't make judgements about my behaviour. I think that's what helped me the most. I can see how regular mindfulness practise is working to keep me calm, focused and centred instead of worrying about things I have no control over. I'm not expending all my energy worrying about things that may not ever happen.

"You did not directly help me with the solutions to my problems but I'm more relaxed and open to ideas, motivated to explore possible solutions myself and with people who matter to me. I was searching on the internet and there are a few apps and online programmes that I can carry on with or use to jog my memory if I'm allowing things to slip. It won't be the same as seeing someone face to face, but it will work as a reminder. Anyway, thank you, Jonathan; I'm grateful for your patience and support."

"It's been a pleasure, Malcolm. Remember to make the most of the moment in the here and now and I hope you live your life mindfully with awareness. Goodbye and take good care of yourself!"

*****

MORE ON MINDFULNESS

Mindfulness encapsulates formal and informal practices that help individuals to be more present and aware internally of their thoughts, feelings and physical body as well as externally of other people and the environment.

Generally, the evidence shows that mindfulness is a safe intervention. However, please consult your doctors prior to engaging in the programme and it should not be applied with anyone who has a chronic mental health condition of a psychotic nature, epilepsy, asthma or high blood pressure.

The most common benefits of practising mindfulness are:

- stress reduction
- more resilience
- improved concentration
- better sleep
- clarity and focus

Five benefits of mindfulness documented in clinical research are:

- stress reduction
- improved relationships
- improved rapport and communication
- greater confidence and self-esteem
- enhanced creativity

There are seven attitudes of Mindfulness:

Non-judgement – This is impartially observing and letting go of the habit of labelling what we experience as good, bad or neutral. By being more aware of these judgements, we can make more informed, conscious choices, instead of merely reacting automatically. Letting go of judgements such as 'boring' can help us sustain and enhance our mindfulness practise. It can also help us to be more accepting of people from different cultures and backgrounds.

Patience – Things unfold and happen at their own natural pace. By understanding this, we can avoid wasting energy and becoming agitated when we fall short of our unrealistic expectations. Patience is helpful in managing our mindfulness practise, as well as in everyday life.

Beginner's Mind – This attitude is best described by the behaviour of children as they view objects, people and experiences for the first time with intrigue and curiosity. As adults, it is about looking at things with fresh eyes as if looking at things for the first time and letting go of previous baggage. This makes us more receptive to new possibilities and fresh perspectives. In the context of mindfulness practise, it is about approaching each session as a new unique experience without pre-conceived notions from past practises.

Trust – We all have an inner wisdom and this attitude is about tuning into and trusting this. It is about trusting this 'sixth sense' when making decisions, instead of always allowing an outside authority to influence our decisions. This might also be thought of as intuition. Mindfulness helps to tune into this 'sixth sense' and inner wisdom.

Non-striving – This is about remaining unattached to outcome and achievement. Enjoying the journey rather than becoming fixated on the destination, which takes the joy out of the journey. We may set goals but also try to let go of the outcome and remain present in each day and moment. In the context of Mindfulness, it is possible to reach goals by not trying to change the present but by being open to whatever arises, and in that way finding that goals are ultimately reached in a variety of ways. Sometimes this can be hard to comprehend, and we need to trust the experience to fully grasp the concept. This is the same for Mindfulness practise. We aim to be fully immersed in the exercise, rather than expecting to feel relaxed, or more focused at the end.

Acceptance – Acceptance does not mean approval or resignation but rather being open and accepting of things as they are. This helps us let go of denial, prejudice and fear. In Mindfulness, it is about accepting each practise just as it is, without criticism.

Letting Go – This is about putting aside the tendency to elevate or reject some aspects of our experiences in life or in Mindfulness practise. Letting things be as they are rather than how they were or should be. This attitude is best understood by feeling the impact and consequences of doing the opposite. Try holding fervently to a belief, object or goal and feeling the relief and liberation of letting go of that rigid mindset.

(Adapted from work by Jon Kabat-Zinn)

Mindfulness can be practised formally or informally. Formal practice is when we set time aside to practise specific meditations like the body scan or three-minute breathing techniques. Informal is the application of mindfulness concepts into everyday activities like eating, walking, having a shower, etc.

Flow state is when we are fully emerged in an activity and giving it our 100% attention and exclusive focus and experience a sense of blissful awareness, inner satisfaction, and being at one with the universe. Examples of activities where flow state is experienced can be running, meditation, music or when children are immersed in play.

Story 11: The New Man

"The benefits of our course are peace of mind, feeling calm and relaxed, improved performance and decision-making."

Neil Arthur, Area Director of Breswell Group Engineering, was reading the content of a newsletter forwarded to him by his deputy, Richard. The newsletter was from a well-known Stress Management and Wellbeing company. Reading the newsletter made him recall a conversation with Richard from a few weeks ago:

"What's wrong, Boss? I've noticed that you have not been yourself for the past few months. Hope you don't mind me asking, but is everything okay?"

"Oh, did not realise it was that obvious. There's just too much going on at work and at home at the minute. I am not sleeping, our new targets are playing on my mind, as well as problems with Mila at home. Can't really share this with our Mr Breswell."

"Ha, give it a try. What's the worst that can happen?" Richard asked.

"He'll say I am a wimp and to get on with it, which is what I am trying to do. To be honest, Rich, I feel as if I'm at breaking point and not sure how long I can keep this up." Neil's eyes welled up.

"You need some help. I'll forward you this email that I got from a Stress Management and Wellbeing firm. I looked at their website and it might be just what you need. Give it a try."

"Come on, Rich, that sort of stuff is all airy-fairy and what do I say to our Mr B?" Neil exclaimed.

"Neil, I'm worried about you. You said yourself that you're at breaking point. I am glad we can talk about this. I'll forward you the email, have a think about it."

Since that conversation two months ago, Neil had read the email several times, subscribed to further newsletters from the company and sent off for their brochure. He read the content again.

'The benefits are peace of mind, feeling calm and relaxed, improved performance and decision-making.'

"I haven't felt at peace for a long time," thought Neil.

He let out a long sigh and read the brochure again, then picked up his phone and dialled the number on it.

It was four weeks later and the office clock had just ticked round to 4pm. Neil grabbed his laptop and briefcase. "It's been a long month. I can't wait to get out of this office," he thought, feeling exhausted and weighed down.

As he walked out, for a brief moment his eyes rested on the picture on his desk. It was of a young woman with finely chiselled cheek bones, large sultry eyes and full mouth curled up in a soft smile. How on earth had he managed to get with a woman as attractive and beautiful as Mila?

"Hey, Neil!" Richard was speeding up to catch up with him before he made it to the exit door. "Breswell has just called and let rip on the phone; he's not happy, we've not hit the performance targets for the third month running."

"Not now, Rich, not now. I'm already late getting away. This will have to wait until I'm back from my holiday next week."

"But, Neil..." Richard's raised voice trailed behind Neil.

"No buts, Rich, this time I am not cancelling my leave to please Mr B!"

Neil carried on toward the exit door. He did not see Sharon the receptionist's puzzled face, and ignored her question, "Are you okay, Mr Arthur?" He frowned at the big sign that shouted at him from above the front door, BRESWELL GROUP. He was looking forward to not having to look at that sign for a few days.

He headed swiftly to the car park, got in his car and set off. A wave of relief swept through him as the barrier to the car park lifted to let him out of the complex. A few fleeting minutes on the road and the memory of Richard's anxious face and the urgency in his voice took over.

"For goodness sake, why is it so hard to put myself first? I need this break and deserve this rest. Do I need to have a nervous breakdown before someone understands?"

Neil ranted to himself and carried on driving. The busyness of the motorway added to his irritability. Everyone on the road seemed to be in a rush, from the lorry drivers in the slow lane to the executives talking into their hands-free sets in their expensive company cars. The bleak grey of the tarmac stretched ahead of him relentlessly until another hour later, when Neil took the exit from the motorway signposted North Wales.

As he drove along the flowing and winding roads, he did not notice the breathtaking beauty of the landscape with shades of orange and yellow which stretched ahead of him beyond the horizon. All he could think of was the consequences of not meeting his departmental targets and the massive overspend on his budget. Mila, his wife, crept up in his thoughts too and he was overwhelmed by a feeling of emptiness within him. Neil rolled down his window, letting in the crisp fragrant breeze which tingled his skin.

The tension in his body had just begun its slow journey of oozing out when he arrived at his destination. As he turned into the drive, he noticed the mountains in the horizon. On the left was a big, blue, two-storey building with large windows. He followed the sign to the car park and reception.

"Welcome," said the young lady on reception. She seemed to be extremely happy, which perturbed Neil, but she was efficient at her job. After the checking-in process, she added, "The stress management course starts at 9.30 am in the Upper Suite; it's just down the corridor on the left. Have a pleasant evening."

This was Hill Valley Retreat, nestled in the heart of the Welsh mountains. As he walked to his room, he looked out at the setting sun as it gently dropped behind the mountains. He paused and took a deep breath, longing for the peace and stillness that had evaded him, not just lately, but for years. After a few seconds, he realised that a few deep breaths were not going to erase the build-up of years of stress in his body. He did not have the energy to go to the introductory dinner that evening, so decided to skip that and have an early night.

An hour later, he lay in bed tossing and turning, peace and stillness still eluding him. "What am I doing here? Should I have seen Mr Breswell before I left? Will this course help me? Will I be able to face my issues? What has my life been about? Why am I always upsetting Mila? Why am I not happy in my career?"

The next day, Neil sat in the last row behind the other twelve delegates on the course listening to Marc, the course facilitator. There was a wisdom and warmth to his words. He was talking about the concept of the 'Stress Pot'; the filling up of unexpressed painful emotions in the body over a period of time.

Marc explained, "As children, and even as adults, when we are not able to process difficult experiences, they store up in the body and can cause health problems. It is important to identify the related emotions and process these using safe techniques."

As he listened to Marc and joined in discussions with the others, he comprehended how he had thrown himself into work to distract from and avoid all his painful feelings to the detriment of his wellbeing. The feeling of exhaustion had crept up on him as his 'stress pot' had filled up over the years with anger and sadness.

"So, how do you spill the stuff out of the pot?" a delegate asked.

Marc replied, "The activity of engaging and talking about your feelings, releases them from the body. Also, writing them down freely, without stopping the ebb, is another way. It may sound hard to do at first, but it is harder and more harmful to hold them in the body in the long term. We will also practise relaxation and other gentler techniques tomorrow which help to do the same."

In the afternoon session of the second day, Marc explained how the traumas of earlier years can be replayed in adult life when the significant people in one's life have similar traits. He asked the delegates to pair up and discuss this. Neil listened to the lady sitting next to him, a marketing manager called Jenny, who shared that she had been fostered at the age of five and her fear that anyone she loves will be taken away from her. She talked of the anger and sadness of not having the love of her alcoholic mother. Other people shared their experiences of being bullied, labelled as stupid, losing loved ones and dealing with discrimination. Neil thought of his dad but was unable to open up to Jenny.

The evening sun moved in and out of the clouds, painting the sky in glorious shades of red. Neil sat by a small pond next to the retreat. He watched the light being reflected in the water, and as the insights from the day occupied his mind, his attention drifted away from the water. His thought train wandered uncontrollably into his past and life at home as a child.

"You've seen me work hard in my room for my maths and science exams every night, Dad; I don't know how I didn't pass." He recalled the terror in his voice as an eleven-year-old.

"No son of a headmaster fails exams; have you no regard for my reputation?" Mr Arthur senior glared at his son and raised his hand, ready to strike.

As Neil recoiled in horror at this memory, it made him think of Mr Breswell, the company owner, who would glare at him in the same way. He was a very old-fashioned manager. It was his way or no way. The company was a success but it was hard to get along with him. In fact, for Neil, it was becoming impossible.

"No manager of mine fails to meet my targets. I have my company reputation to maintain."

Every time Mr Breswell's small, grey, beady eyes bored into him, Neil's stomach knotted up in terror.

"I am still trying to get my dad's approval!" Neil was struck with this awareness. "I must stop doing that and do what is right by me!" He hurried to his room, grabbed a writing pad and began to write out his anger towards his father.

"Dad, I am so angry at you because..." The anger did somersaults in his stomach until it eventually subsided. He fought through it and continued to write. An hour later Neil lay on the couch, feeling a lot better having released his demons. "I must do this every time I'm angry with something and not store it in my stress pot," he thought.

On the morning of the third day, Neil sat in the front row, eager to fill in more pieces of his life puzzle. He listened to Marc intently.

"A good indication of when we have emptied our stress pot of the negative feelings is when we are ready to forgive ourselves and others for those experiences. When someone holds onto negative emotions, it does more harm to the self than to the other person. Therefore, forgiveness is more about our healing and recovery."

Story 11: The New Man

Neil felt comfortable about opening up to the other delegates in their small discussion groups. As he talked and shared more, he felt a great weight lift from his shoulders. Neil also realised how his relationship with his dad had shaped the way he related to others, wanting to keep control of them.

That evening, with more of his life puzzle pieces falling into place, Neil sat down to send two very important emails. Part of his email to Mr Breswell read:

"I know I haven't been at my best lately, but I just wanted to let you know that my head's in the right place now and I want to do my best for the Group. Can we arrange a meeting when I return?"

He wrote a second email to his wife which said:

"Mila, please forgive me. I know that I have not been fair to you, bullying you to be what I want you to be, like my dad and Mr Breswell wanted to make me. That is the only way I knew to relate to someone. You can only be what you are, not what someone wants you to be. We need to have a serious talk about us and our future. I want to be a better person."

On the fourth and last day, Marc led several relaxation practices. Neil fully allowed himself to be immersed in the tranquillity of the process. This time the peace and stillness stayed with him throughout the day. "I have never felt so relaxed in all my life! How can I maintain this feeling after today?"

Marc guided him to the retreat in-house shop and the books, audio and visual products that the delegates could use themselves after the course.

"I am at peace with myself a little," thought Neil as he packed up and walked out to the car park. He caught his image in the mirror as he got into the car and looked at himself in surprise. "There is something new about me," he thought. He could not put his finger on what was different, but he could not stop looking at himself in the mirror. He seemed to have less lines on his forehead and noticed a change in his facial expression. Gone was the permanent frown. Instead, he had more of a relaxed, at-ease expression on his face.

On his drive back home, he turned up the radio and sang out aloud, something he had not done for a long time. He used to sing to himself at his desk, until Mr Breswell told him not to.

"Mr B needs to learn to relax and enjoy himself," thought Neil. He mentally composed an email to Mr Breswell, pointing out how he could do this.

Neil thought of all the changes in his own life that he could make to ensure he did not have a nervous breakdown and avoid long-term sick absence.

"I need to do my relaxation practice every day, not bottle up my frustrations but write them out, and open up communication with Mila and Mr Breswell."

When he joined the motorway, he carried on with the singing, oblivious of the funny looks other drivers were giving him.

The following week when Neil came into work, he breezed past Sharon and much to her surprise, offered a warm "Good morning and how are you?" He carried on towards his office with strength in his stride, a glow in his face and a twinkle in his eyes. As he entered his office, Mila's face smiled at him from the picture on his desk. He smiled back at her beautiful face, his heart filling up with love and tenderness.

Richard popped his head round his office door.

"Hey, Rich, everything okay? I will see you later at 11am for a chat," said Neil.

"Okay, Neil, good to have you back. How was your holiday?"

"Amazing, just amazing. I feel like a new man," chimed Neil. "Please can you set up a meeting with Mr Breswell, tomorrow if possible?"

"Ah... talking of which, he said he wanted to see you as soon as you were in," Richard replied. Neil decided that he better go and see Mr Breswell straight away, so he headed for his office.

"I got your email while you were away. What the hell is going on? You did not reply to my messages and I found these brochures on your desk last week. Want to tell me what this is all about?"

Neil explained in great depth how he had spent a few days at Hill Valley Retreat, why he went, how he had found out so much about himself and how he now felt like a new man.

"A new man, you say?" Mr Breswell ran his finger down the spine of one of the brochures. "Well, get back to work and let's see what that really means."

What it really meant was that Neil was more focused on his work and better able to relate and communicate with his staff. He was working smarter as he made decisions swiftly and increased his effectiveness at the end of the day. He was also thinking about using the methods that Marc had given him to enhance the reputation of Breswell's.

It was about time for Mr B to also think about changing into a new man!

*****

MORE ON STRESS MANAGEMENT

Neil's scenario is a good example of how excessive stress can seriously impact work performance. On an organisational level, it is imperative that employers and managers manage stress in the workplace to stop situations such as Neil's from escalating. In the case of Neil, stress led to poor performance until he was proactive in seeking help. If it is not addressed, at its worst stress in the workplace can lead to critical mistakes being made, sickness absence and ultimately a rise in grievances. It can also have a knock-on effect on other members of staff and lead to a decrease in staff morale.

In the UK, managers have a legal duty to address stress issues and the welfare of their employees under the Health and Safety Legislation. Businesses that neglect this duty often do not realise the long-term cost of this on all levels; profits, reputation and moral implications. Mr Breswell was not paying attention and was unaware of the costs to his company if Neil had gone off on long-term sick absence.

Some of the consequences of this would have been:

- Cost of lost productivity while Neil was off sick
- Cost of replacing him with temporary staff
- Loss of Neil's skills and expertise and commitment to his company

- Potential complaints from customers
- Extra workload and pressure on Richard and the rest of team

Managers need to know how to spot signs of stress amongst employees. The best way of doing this is to have an open, trusting relationship with members of staff and encourage them to talk about any issues they may have. Good communication processes that generate a culture where there is no stigma attached to talking about stress is imperative. Having a stress policy and format for stress risk assessments will also help to have a framework for ensuring that all cases of stress are dealt with appropriately.

Neil did not feel able to talk to Mr Breswell because the culture that Mr Breswell had built did not make that possible.

As for Neil on an individual level, it took him a long time to realise that he needed to seek help in order to alleviate his stress. Acknowledging that you are experiencing high stress levels is the first important step towards dealing with the problem. If ignored, excessive stress will affect your physical health, behaviour, ability to make decisions, your relationships and how you perform at work.

Can you identify with any of the following indicators of excessive stress?

Physical Signs

- High blood pressure
- Nervous speech
- Panic attacks
- Tiredness/Lethargy
- Upset stomach
- Tension headaches
- Hand tremors
- Rapid weight gain/loss
- Constantly feeling cold
- Chest palpitations

Work Performance

- Any change in performance
- Uncharacteristic errors
- Loss of control over work
- Loss of motivation
- Indecision
- Cutting corners
- Absenteeism/Presenteeism
- Not taking holidays
- Bullying
- Criticising others

Emotional Signs and Thoughts

- Anger outbursts
- Short temper
- Crying/Weeping
- Depression/Anxiety
- Panic attacks
- Fear of criticism
- Feeling out of control
- Loss of confidence
- Cluttered thinking
- Memory lapses
- Slow decision-making
- Difficulty in concentrating

Behavioural Signs

- Out of character behaviour
- Difficulty in relaxing
- Increased alcohol/smoking
- Recreational drug use
- Neglect appearance/hygiene
- Bored
- Unnecessary risk-taking
- Frustrated
- Unmotivated/Apathetic

If you find that some of them apply to you, then you are displaying signs of excessive stress. If ignored, this may lead to long-term adverse effects on relationships, your physical health and your long-term direction in life. Acknowledge this and seek help. Often taking simple steps and persevering with it will turn things around, as it did for Neil.

Neil found the 'stress pot' concept to be a great help. He learnt to 'empty' his stress pot by writing out his built-up feelings and through relaxation techniques.

Here are some of the other methods that Neil used to de-stress on a regular basis that you may want to try.

Focus on your body relaxation
Slowly scan your body and relax all your muscles. Tell your face to relax, then your neck, shoulders, arms, chest, abdomen, back, hips, legs, feet and toes. Tell yourself to let go of the tension as you focus on each area of your body. Finally allow your whole body to relax. When you have finished, think of yourself as relaxed and calm. "I am relaxed and calm for the rest of the day."

Simple meditation
Sit comfortably in a quiet place with your arms and legs uncrossed and breathe gently for a few minutes. Then choose a positive word that resonates for you (e.g. relax, calm, peace, love, etc.). Traditionally, the mantra "Om" or "Aum" is used in meditation so you may want to use that.

Silently repeat this word slowly. Your mind will wander off sometimes and that is normal. As soon as you notice that this has happened, gently bring your attention to the positive word that you have chosen to anchor your meditation and continue with this practice for ten to thirty minutes. Open your eyes and stay seated for a few more minutes before engaging in activity.

Object meditation

Choose a beautiful object like a flower arrangement, tranquil picture or sight, lighted candle, etc. Focus your attention on it steadily. Study the detail of the object, the colours, shapes, shades, etc. Do this for five to ten minutes, then close your eyes and visualise the object, its shape and features. This is especially good for improving your concentration.

Summary

I hope you have been inspired by these stories and they have galvanised your journey to optimum wellbeing as well as empowered you to make changes within your business and/or personal life.

As you have gathered, stress is a very common factor in our lives; in fact, you could go as far as to say it is part of the human condition. Unmanaged stress levels can build until it upsets the balance of our lives, affecting our work, relationships, happiness and health.

This can be demonstrated well by using the metaphor of an aeroplane. Imagine your life or your organisation as a wonderful state-of-the-art aeroplane. Every stage, from drawing board to the sky, has taken the talents of hundreds of people. However, metal, that resilient, miraculous material, can suffer from metal fatigue and the aircraft must be checked regularly for signs, as one overstressed piece of aluminium is enough to bring a plane down. It is the same for our human body. So watch out for the first signs and draw on the concepts and techniques in these stories to build your resilience and wellbeing.

These stories illustrate the enormous importance of recognising when we need help. There is, as Jonathan reminds Malcolm in one of the stories, not a sign of weakness or shame in seeking out support; quite the contrary – it shows wisdom and strength.

Integrate one wellness action and build on this each week over a period until you are feeling completely at peace with yourself, joyful and rejuvenated. The aim is to sustain this state of being for the rest of your life to optimise success in your personal and professional life, which may seem impossible but can be achieved.

Similarly, introducing gradual changes at work can lead to a more engaged, healthy workforce, boost productivity and save money lost by those stressful situations as well as create a caring and thriving culture.

Feel free to contact us if you need support in achieving this goal.

www.aumconsultancy.co.uk
or text **+44(0)7888747438**

Please leave a review on Amazon or our website to help us, to help more people and organisations on their wellness journeys.

Acknowledgements

It goes without saying that my husband and children continue to be by my side with all my life endeavours.

However, I would like in the main to pay tribute to all my clients; the ones I have worked with individually and those in group and corporate settings. This book was inspired by their unique stories and experiences.

Thanks also to all my associates (we too are like one big happy family) and especially to Marc Kirby for his contribution to The Mediator story and Kristina Rosenqvist for her valuable feedback. A mega thank you to my editors: Olivia Eisinger, Zara Thatcher and Desi Binyon.

Heartfelt thanks to my dear friend Jackie Jones and my business manager, Simon Day. This book would not have been possible without their encouragement and belief in the value of the stories.

Finally, I owe thanks to the universal forces that guide me and keep me on my true path.

Other books by Hansa Pankhania

Stress to Success in 28 days – A Unique Programme for Total Wellbeing

Hansa brings together all the tools and techniques for wellbeing and stress prevention that she has accumulated over her twenty-five-year career. She skilfully presents these in a twenty-eight-day programme for individuals and managers to propel healthy living and wellbeing.

Best of Three Worlds – a soulful, cultural and historical journey across three continents

In her memoir, Hansa talks about the values, experiences, mindfulness principles and practices that have helped her to deal with the stressful times in her life and sustain wellbeing, resilience and creativity. The lessons learned and practices she adopts are from three continents from which her ancestors originate.

Children's Books

Chakraji and Calm Callum
Chakraji and Relaxed Ravina
Chakraji and Peaceful Peter

A trilogy of wellbeing books for children and adults
Hansa's three children's books are the tales of children's journeys to meet the magical Chakraji. The stories use imaginative storytelling, to help children articulate and manage stressful situations. It's ideal for children and parents to manage everyday tensions and mitigate mental health issues later in life.

Also soon to be published

Chakraji and Beautiful Bella
Chakraji and Marvellous Mansoor
Chakraji and Special Sue Ling

About the Author

Hansa Pankhania is the Founder of AUM WELLBEING CONSULTANCY

She is immensely proud of her job as an **Author, Executive Coach and Speaker**, and cherishes the opportunity to support the world in managing the stress and anxiety that is prevalent in society today. Her passion is to pass on powerful, natural stress relief techniques to managers, adults and children to prevent mental health issues and enable healthy and happy living.

In her corporate role, she is an expert in Manager and Corporate Wellbeing and Resilience, having worked in this field for the past twenty-five years, and offered coaching and consultancy to over 300 companies, countless managers, and employees.

Her mission is to help companies save money lost through stressful situations, and develop mindful, conscious and trusting workplace environments to maximise potential and profits.

She has published seven books on this topic, including a series of *Stress to Success* books. Her memoir *Best of Three Worlds* talks about the values, experiences, mindfulness principles and practices that have helped her to deal with the stressful times in her life and sustain wellbeing, resilience and purpose. The lessons learned and practices she adopts are from Kenya, India and England, three countries from which her ancestors originate.

Her latest series of CHAKRAJI children's books uses imaginative storytelling, helping children to manage stress using natural interventions.

She has a national and international team of associates who offer Coaching and Consultancy for Individuals and Managers on Wellbeing and Stress Prevention and are committed to developing mindful, compassionate, thriving workplace cultures.

For more information visit **www.aumconsultancy.co.uk**
Or text **+44(0)7888747438**

9 781914 201141